Consider the following testimony of an emigrant, given before a justice in Albany. He says that "in June last, the parish officers paid the passages of himself and about forty others of the same parish, from Chatham to the city of Boston, in America, on board the ship Royalist, Capt. Parker, and that they landed in Boston in the month of July last, that the parish officers gave him thirty shillings sterling, in money, in addition to paying his passage—that he is now entirely destitute of the means of living, and is unable to labor, and prays for relief."

—Samuel F.B. Morse

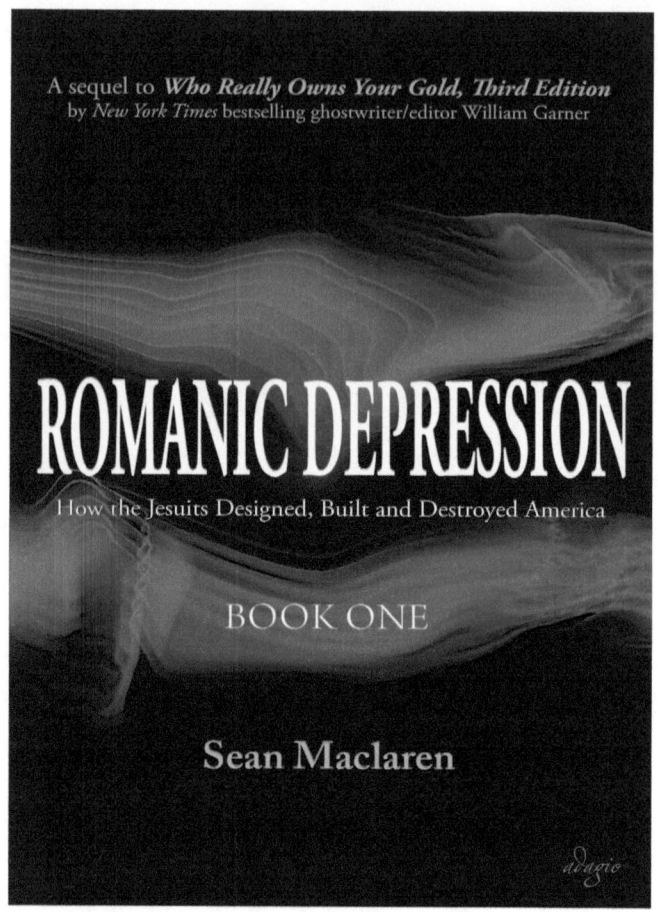

Romanic Depression
Available from Amazon.com and other bookstores

eBook available from Amazon.com, AdagioPress.com and WilliamDeanAGarner.com

The first book in a four-part series that reveals how the Jesuits have designed, built and destroyed every sector of American society, from Law and Government to Politics to Healthcare to Education. Also with more than 200 excellent references.

Edited by William Dean A. Garner
New York Times bestselling ghostwriter/editor

The Suppressed Truth
About the Assassination of Abraham Lincoln
Available from Amazon.com and other bookstores

eBook available from Amazon.com, AdagioPress.com and WilliamDeanAGarner.com

Burke McCarty was a courageous ex-Catholic who conducted diligent research on the details surrounding the murder of President Abraham Lincoln by the Jesuits.

Edited by William Dean A. Garner
New York Times bestselling ghostwriter/editor

Machiavelli's *The Prince*
Available from Amazon.com and other bookstores

eBook available from Amazon.com, AdagioPress.com and
WilliamDeanAGarner.com

The Prince is a raw and bloody field manual for upper- and mid-level managers on predatorial ethics and power: what it is, how to obtain it, and what to do with it once you have found, stumbled across, or been granted it.

Edited by William Dean A. Garner
New York Times bestselling ghostwriter/editor

Sun Tzu *The Art of War*
Available from Amazon.com and other bookstores

eBook available from Amazon.com, AdagioPress.com and WilliamDeanAGarner.com

This contemporary edition of Sun Tzu's timeless masterpiece is just as, if not more, relevant today as it was 2,500 years ago, and is wholly effective on the battlefield, and in the boardroom and bedroom. The wisdom of *The Art of War* teaches us that war is unnecessary. Peace is always the goal.

Edited by William Dean A. Garner
New York Times bestselling ghostwriter/editor

The Escape and Suicide of
John Wilkes Booth
The Jesuit Assassin of Abraham Lincoln
Available from Amazon.com and other bookstores

eBook available from Amazon.com, AdagioPress.com and WilliamDeanAGarner.com

Researcher, author and attorney Finis L. Bates did exhaustive work to uncover the accurate history about Jesuit assassin John Wilkes Booth after he murdered President Abraham Lincoln.

Edited by William Dean A. Garner
New York Times bestselling ghostwriter/editor

Fifty Years in the Church of Rome
Available from Amazon.com and other bookstores

eBook available from Amazon.com, AdagioPress.com and WilliamDeanAGarner.com

Rev. Charles Chiniquy chronicles his 50 years as a servant of the Church of Rome, while also revealing the evil machinations of the Jesuits and their Roman Catholic minions. He includes information about the assassination of President Abraham Lincoln by the Jesuits, and their controlling the United States and other countries.

Edited by William Dean A. Garner
New York Times bestselling ghostwriter/editor

ARCANUM
A critical analysis of the original 36 sermons of Jmmanuel,
the man known to the world as Jesus Christ
Available from Amazon.com and other bookstores

eBook available from Amazon.com, AdagioPress.com and
WilliamDeanAGarner.com

In Part 1, Maclaren psychoanalyzes Jmmanuel's sermons, which are featured in Part 2. In Part 3, Maclaren reveals The Laws of Creation that Jmmanuel discussed but never actually revealed in depth.

Edited by William Dean A. Garner
New York Times bestselling ghostwriter/editor

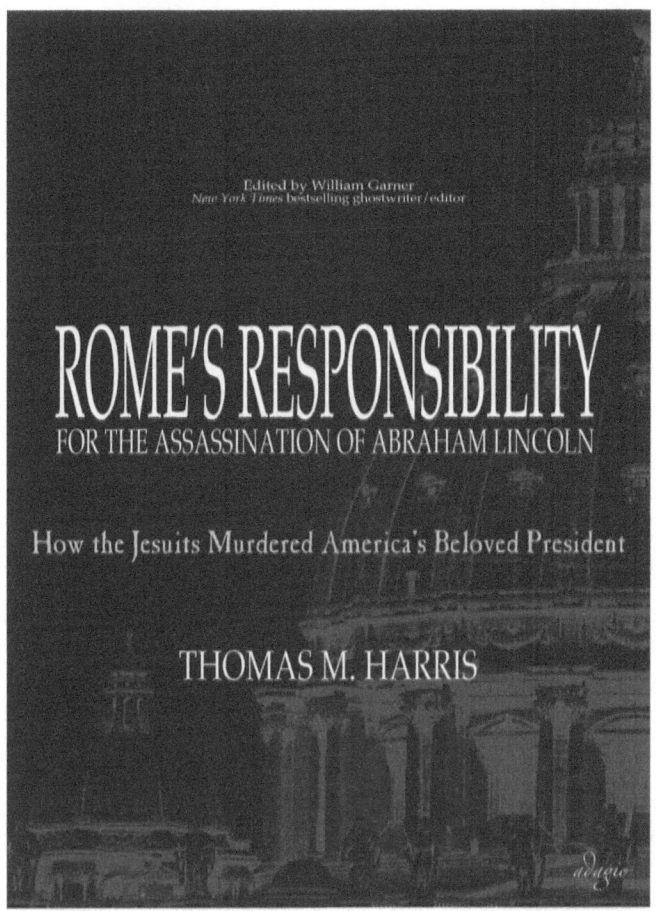

Rome's Responsibility
for the Assassination of Abraham Lincoln
How the Jesuits Murdered America's Beloved President
Available from Amazon.com and other bookstores

eBook available from Amazon.com, AdagioPress.com and
WilliamDeanAGarner.com

General Thomas M. Harris, a member of the Lincoln Assassination Military Commission, details how the Jesuits plotted over many months to murder America's President Abraham Lincoln.

Edited by William Dean A. Garner
New York Times bestselling ghostwriter/editor

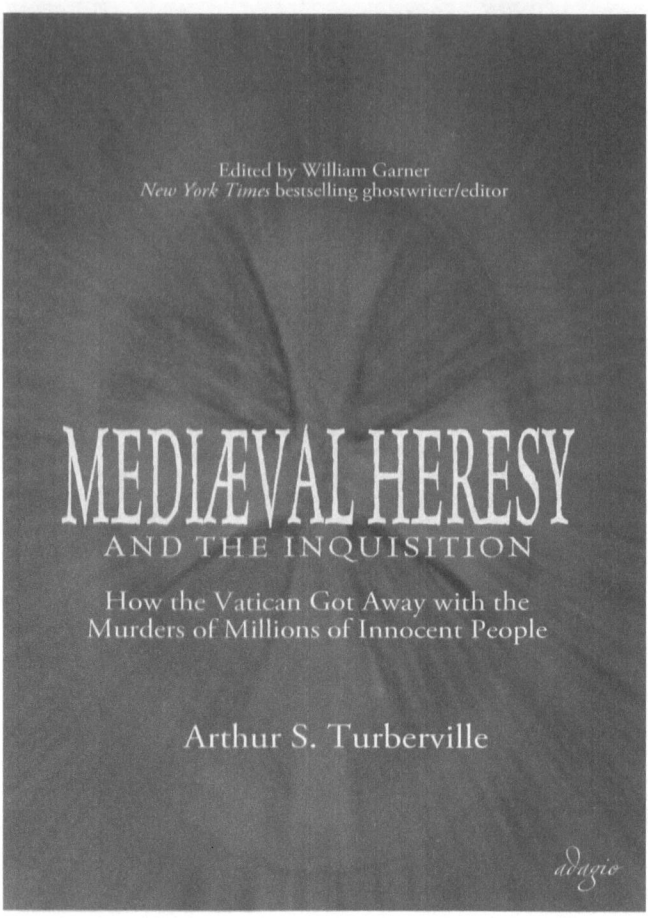

Mediæval Heresy & The Inquisition
How the Vatican Got Away with the Murders of Innocent People
Available from Amazon.com and other bookstores

eBook available from Amazon.com, AdagioPress.com and
WilliamDeanAGarner.com

Arthur S. Turberville published a fairly detailed account of the infamous Roman Inquisition, a medieval method of torture that was designed to punish and discourage all who opposed the Roman Catholic Church's established dogma.

Edited by William Dean A. Garner
New York Times bestselling ghostwriter/editor

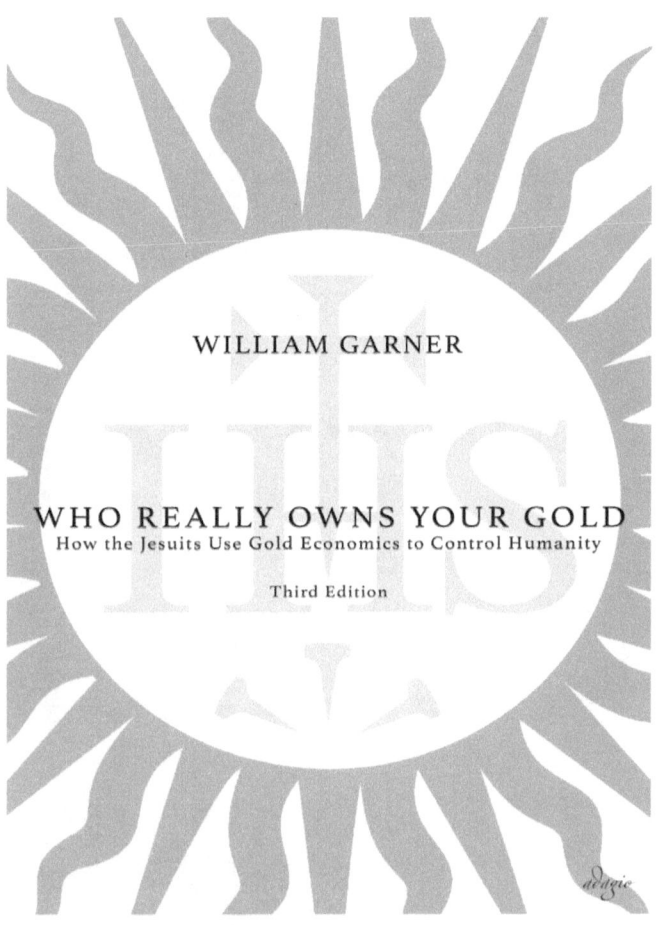

Who Really Owns Your Gold, 3rd Edition

How the Jesuits Use Gold Economics to Control Humanity

Available from Amazon.com and other bookstores

eBook available from Amazon.com, AdagioPress.com and WilliamDeanAGarner.com

Who Really Owns Your Gold, Third Edition, is about much more than just gold economics. It's about the manipulation of every sector of life across the globe by a dynastic group of men in Rome, the Jesuits, who are successfully building a world that is counter to every good belief we hold dear and true.

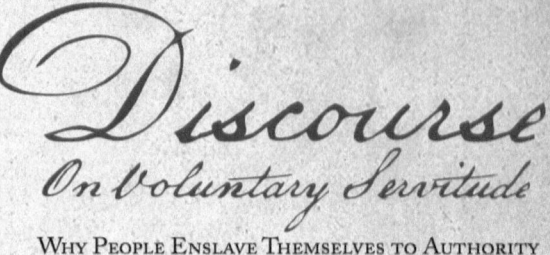

Discourse on Voluntary Servitude
Why People Enslave Themselves to Authority
Available from Amazon.com and other bookstores

eBook available from Amazon.com, AdagioPress.com and
WilliamDeanAGarner.com

Étienne de La Boétie's masterpiece is still highly relevant today. While short in words, it speaks volumes to all those who value liberty on all levels, but who are currently trapped in the yoke of oppression by the many tyrants in every government and institution.

Edited by William Dean A. Garner
New York Times bestselling ghostwriter/editor

VA Disability Claim, 3rd Edition
How to Prepare, File and Maintain a VA Disability Claim and Appeal
Available from Amazon.com and other bookstores

eBook available from Amazon.com, AdagioPress.com and VADisabilityClaimBook.com

VA Disability Claim, Third Edition, has been revamped to reflect the hundreds of suggestions from discerning and caring veterans who commented on the first two editions.

Edited by William Dean A. Garner
New York Times bestselling ghostwriter/editor

How To Write Your First Book
A Simple and Practical Method for Anyone Who Can Tell a Story
Available from Amazon.com and other bookstores

eBook available from Amazon.com, AdagioPress.com and
WilliamDeanAGarner.com

This gem is much more than just a book about writing. It reveals metaphysically how our subconscious functions during the creative process to produce the finished product, and how we grow spiritually as this process evolves before us to create our first book.

Garner employs a simple, step-by-step method we have used all our lives, and includes easy-to-follow examples and exercises, plus anecdotes from his work as a ghostwriter/editor.

The Laws of Creation and The Universe
A Special Gift for Mankind
Available from Amazon.com and other bookstores

eBook available from Amazon.com, AdagioPress.com and WilliamDeanAGarner.com

In his previous book, *Arcanum*, Sean Maclaren dissected the 36 extant sermons of Jmmanuel Sananda, the man known to the world as Jesus Christ, and discovered more than 120 Laws of Creation and The Universe. Those gifts are featured in this current volume.

Edited by William Dean A. Garner
New York Times bestselling ghostwriter/editor

Edited by William Garner
New York Times bestselling Ghostwriter/Editor

FOREIGN CONSPIRACY
AGAINST THE LIBERTIES OF THE UNITED STATES

Samuel F.B. Morse

adagio

AN INDEPENDENT PUBLISHING CRUISE
est. January 1, 2001

Katharine L. Petersen
Publisher / Senior Editor
William Dean A. Garner
Editor

Copyright © 2017 Adagio Press
All rights reserved

Published in America by Adagio Press

Adagio and colophon are Trademarks of Adagio Press

Library of Congress Control Number: 2016921312

ISBN: 978-1-944855-09-3

Adagio website: AdagioPress.com

Cover design and interior: Dean Garner
Cover art: commissioned painting by Ciska Liversage

B20170101
First Print Edition

for You, dear Reader

Recommendations

NEW YORK. Jan. 1, 1835.

Gentlemen,—Learning that you are about to publish in a small volume, the articles signed Brutus (which recently appeared in the *New York Observer*, showing that a conspiracy is formed against the United States by the Papal powers of Europe), the undersigned, who read those articles with interest, have great satisfaction in expressing their approbation of your undertaking. These articles are written by a gentleman of intelligence and candor, who has resided in the south of Europe, and enjoyed the best opportunities for acquaintance with the topics on which he writes.

While we disapprove of harsh, denunciatory language toward Roman Catholics, their past history, and the fact that they everywhere act together, as if guided by one mind, admonish us to be jealous of their influence, and to watch with unremitted care all their movements in relation to our free institutions. As this work is now to be published in a portable form, and with additional notes by the author, we hope it may obtain an extensive circulation and a careful perusal.

Yours, with friendly regard,

JAMES MILNOR, N. BANGS,
THOMAS DE WITT, JONATHAN GOING.

The gentlemen who have signed the above letter represent four Protestant denominations, viz., the Episcopal, Presbyterian, Methodist, and Baptist.

EXTRACT FROM *ZION'S HERALD*, A METHODIST PAPER, PUBLISHED IN BOSTON, MASS.

"FOREIGN CONSPIRACY.—We commence today publishing this interesting series. The author is an American, who has resided for a long time in Italy and Austria. The same day that we had decided to publish them, we received a note, signed by Rev. Messrs. Lindsey, Fillmore, Kent, and Stevens, recommending and requesting that they should appear in the *Herald*."

Recommendations since the Publication of the First Edition.

The author of a little volume just published in this city, entitled *Foreign Conspiracy Against the Liberties of the United States*, is a gentleman personally known to us, and universally esteemed. We commend this volume to the serious attention of all Americans who love liberty, and mean to maintain it.

The author undertakes to show that a conspiracy against the liberties of this Republic is now in full action, under the direction of the wily Prince Metternich of Austria, who, knowing the impossibility of obliterating this troublesome example of a great and free nation by force of arms, is attempting to accomplish his object through the agency of an army of Jesuits. The array of facts and arguments going to prove the existence of such a conspiracy, will astonish any man who opens the book with the same incredulity as we did.

The author has travelled extensively in Europe, has resided many months, if not many years, in Italy, and understands full well the kind of machinery which the politico-religious despots of the Old World would be likely to put in motion for the subversion of our liberties. He has taken hold of the subject with a strong hand, and if he has not proved the existence of a conspiracy, he has certainly proved an immense accumulation of foreign despotic influence among us, particularly in the West, by means of priests and money sent here from foreign despotic countries. And he has further proved, that the personal influence and pecuniary aid of the Emperor of Austria and his principal Minister, as well as many of his subjects, is directed with unceasing assiduity to maintain the foothold they have gained, and to spread the contagion of their doctrines throughout this fair Republic.

We ask again, that if any are disposed to regard this subject as of little importance, they will give to the *Foreign Conspiracy* a serious and attentive perusal. —*N.Y. Journal of Commerce*

The author, well and alike known to us as an accomplished scholar and artist, has recently returned from a European residence of several years, during which period he became in various ways possessed of facts and circumstances inducing him to believe in the real and substantial existence of a conspiracy, which he has attempted to expose. When he commenced his labors, we frankly told him, in repeated conversations, that we were

Recommendations

incredulous of the fact he was maintaining; but we are free to confess that, in the course of his labors he has brought forward a mass of direct and circumstantial testimony, documentary and otherwise, which has left a strong impression upon our minds, that after all, the alarm may not have been sounded without cause. Events have also transpired in our own country, which, in connection with the suspicious movements of exotic prelates, have imparted still greater importance to the writings of Brutus. —*N.Y. Commercial Advertiser*

One excellence of the publication before us, almost peculiar to this writer, when compared to others who have written upon this subject in our country, is, that it handles the matter of discussion with calmness, the writer not suffering himself to indite his letters under the influence of exacerbated feelings, but wisely avoids those harsh and blackening epithets which do more to irritate the passions than to convince and enlighten the judgment. On this account the book may be read with profit by all. —*N.Y. Christian Advocate* (Methodist)

We would briefly observe that the work, as it is now revised and corrected by the author, and illustrated by him with an Appendix of valuable notes, seems to be something almost altogether new, if not as to the substance, at least as it respects its adventitious embellishments and illustrations. The notes of the Appendix may be truly considered as so many rich pearls, which set off a figure already and altogether prepossessing, to the best advantage.

The author manifests the spirit of a Christian on every page; and although he develops a conspiracy the most formidable against our liberties, both civil and religious, not a vindictive breath ruffles the serenity of his mind. He steps forward, conscious of the rectitude of his motives, not to excite a false alarm, but coolly and deliberately to present facts to our view. This work, in regard to its classical merits, is an honor to American genius. The style is smooth, flowing, and mellifluous. It is like a garden whose walks are lined with flowers, where those who would imitate the industry of the bee, may find a rich profusion of varied sweets.

On reading the last chapter of this valuable work, we are struck with the contrast between the pacific disposition of the author, and the ruthless spirit which characterizes the insidious enemy, whose machinations he exposes. —*N.Y. Downfall of Babylon* (Presbyt.)

The letters of Brutus deserve an extensive circulation.
—Missouri, *St. Louis Observer* (Presbyt.)

From what I have seen and know, the fears entertained by the writer in the New York Observer, under the caption of *Foreign Conspiracy*, &c., are not without foundation, especially in the West.
—Letter of a Traveler in the West. (Maryland) Methodist Protestant.

The author maintains, that what is called the Roman Catholic Religion is in reality a political despotism, disguised under a religious name. We think he proves it; and also that the leading enemies of free institutions in Europe are engaged in organized efforts to give that despotism prevalence in the United States.

The author has not given his name; but it may not be amiss to state that he has been intimately acquainted with Popery in Europe. We do not believe that the progress of Popery in this country can be checked effectually in any way but by the conversion of its votaries. The Gospel must be preached to the Catholic emigrant, and by its influence he must be brought to repent and believe. And it seems evident to us, that the political argument is, from its very nature, incapable of exciting men to the effort by which this can be accomplished.

Preaching the Gospel from political considerations will not convert men. We think that writers on Popery have been too unmindful of this truth. Yet the political argument, like all truth, has its value, and ought not to be neglected. In this work it is admirably presented. We hope it will be widely circulated and attentively read.
—Massachusetts, *Boston Recorder* (Congregational).

Brutus has published his *Conspiracy*, &c., in a small volume, accompanied with notes. They are elaborate and eloquent articles. I hope it will be scattered over the whole country. He is a distinguished scholar and artist of this city, and has his information from personal observation, while in Europe a few years since. —Letter to the Editor of the Mass. *Zion's Herald* (Methodist.)

The numbers of Brutus.—Our readers are already acquainted with their contents. The object is to awaken the attention of the American public

Recommendations

to a design, supposed to be entertained by the despotic governments of Europe, particularly of Austria, in conjunction with his Holiness the Pope, to undermine gradually our free institutions by the promotion of the Catholic religion in America.

The letters are interesting from the numerous facts which they disclose; and are deserving the careful attention of the citizens of these United States, who should guard with vigilance the sacred trust which has been confided to us by our fathers. —*N.Y. Weekly Messenger*

Brutus.—The able pieces over this signature, relative to the designs of Catholicity in our highly favored land, originally published in the *New York Observer*, it is now ascertained were written, not by an individual who was barely indulging in conjectures, but by one who has witnessed the Papacy in all its deformity. One who has, not long since, travelled extensively in the Romish countries, and has spent much time in the Italian States, where the seat of the Beast is.

Rome is familiar to him, and he has watched the movements there with great particularity. We may, therefore, yield a good degree of credence to what Brutus has told us. His numbers are now published in a Pamphlet, and the fact which has just come out in regard to his peculiar qualification to write on this great subject, will give them extensive circulation. —*Utica Baptist Register*

The work embodies a mass of facts, collected from authentic sources, of the deepest interest to every friend of civil liberty and Protestant Christianity. The efforts of despotic European sovereigns, to inoculate our country with the religion of Rome, are fully proved. Could they succeed in these efforts, and annihilate the spirit of liberty on our shores, the march of free principles in our own dominions would cease. They could then sit securely on their thrones, and rule with a rod of iron over their abject vassals. —Ohio, *Cincinnati Journal* (Presbyt.)

Contents

Preface to the Second Edition x
Prefatory Remarks xxiv

Chapter I: 1

The first impression of the improbability of foreign conspiracy considered • Present political condition of Europe favors an enterprise against our institutions • The war of opinions commenced • Despotism against Liberty • The vicissitudes of this war • The official declaration of the despotic party against all liberty • Necessity to the triumph of despotism, that American liberty should be destroyed • The kind of attack upon us most likely to be adopted from the nature of the contest • Particular reasons why our institutions are obnoxious to the European governments • Has the attack commenced? Yes! By Austria, through a Society called the *St. Leopold Foundation* • Ostensibly religious in its designs

Chapter II: 8

Political character of the Austrian government, the power attacking us • The old avowed enemy of Protestant liberty • Character of the *people* of Austria • Slaves • Character of Prince Metternich, the arch-contriver of plans to stifle liberty • These enemies of all liberty suddenly anxious for the *civil and religious liberty* of the United States • The absurdity of their ostensible design exposed • The avowed objects of Austria in the *Leopold* Foundation • Popery the instrument to act upon our institutions

Chapter III: 13

Popery, in its *political*, not its *religious* character, the object of the present examination • The fitness of the instrument to accomplish the political designs of despotism considered • The principles of a *despotic* and *free* government briefly contrasted • Despotic principles fundamental in Popery • Proved by infallible testimony • Papal claims of *divine right* and *plenitude of power* • Abject principles of Popery illustrated from the Russian catechism • Protestantism from its birth in favor of liberty • Luther on the 4th of July attacked the presumptuous claim of divine right • Despotism and Popery hand in hand against the liberty of conscience, liberty of opinion, and liberty of the press • The anti-republican declarations of the present Pope Gregory XVI.

Contents

Chapter IV: 21

The cause of Popery and despotism identical • Striking difference between Popery and Protestantism as they exist in this country • American Protestantism not controlled by Foreign Protestantism • American Popery entirely under foreign control • Jesuits, the Foreign agents of Austria, bound by the strongest ties of interest to Austrian policy, not to American • Their dangerous power • unparalleled in any Protestant sect • Our free institutions opposed in their nature to the arbitrary claims of Popery • Duplicity to be expected • Political dangers to be apprehended from Roman Catholic organization • American Roman Catholic ecclesiastical matters uncontrolled by Americans or in America; managed in a foreign country, by a foreign power, for political purposes • Consequences that may easily result from such a state of things

Chapter V: 25

Points in our political system which favor this foreign attack • Our toleration of all religious systems • Popery opposed to all toleration • Charge of intolerance substantiated • The organization of Popery in America connected with, and strengthened by foreign organization • Without a parallel among Protestant sects • Great preponderance of Popish strength in consequence • The divisions among Protestant sects nullifies their attempts at combination • Taken advantage of by Jesuits • Popish duplicity illustrated in its opposite alliances in Europe with despotism, and in America with democracy • The laws relating to *emigration* and *naturalization* favor foreign attack • Emigrants being mostly Catholic, and in entire subjection to their priests • No remedy provided by our laws for this alarming evil

Chapter VI: 30

The evil from emigration further considered • Its political bearings • The influence of emigrants at the elections • This influence concentrated in the priests • The priests must be propitiated • By what means • This influence easily purchased by the demagogue • The unprincipled character of many of our politicians favor this foreign attack • Their bargain for the suffrages of this priest-led band • A church and state party • The Protestant sects obnoxious to no such bargaining • The newspaper press favors this foreign attack • From its want of independence and its timidity • An anti-republican fondness for titles favors this foreign attack • Cautious attempts of Popery to dignify its emissaries, and to accustom us to their high-sounding titles • A mistaken notion on the subject of discussing *religious* opinion in the secular journals favors this foreign attack • Political designs not to be shielded from attack because cloaked by religion

Chapter VII: 37

The *political* character of this ostensibly *religious* enterprise proved from the letters of the Jesuits now in this country • Their antipathy to *private judgment* • Their anticipations of a change in our form of government • Our government declared too free for the exercise of their divine rights • Their political partialities • Their cold acknowledgment of the generosity, and liberality, and hospitality of our government • Their estimate of our condition contrasted with their estimate of that of Austria • Their acknowledged allegiance and servility to a foreign master • Their sympathies with the oppressor, and not with the oppressed • Their direct avowal of *political* intention

CHAPTER VIII: 43

Some of the means by which Jesuits can already operate *politically* in the country • By mob discipline • By *priest police* • Then great danger • Already established • Proofs • Priests already rule the mob • Nothing in the principles of Popery to prevent its interference in our elections • Popery interferes at the present day in the politics of other countries • Popery the same in our country • It interferes in our elections • In Michigan, Charleston, S.C., and New York • Popery a political despotism cloaked under the name of Religion • It is Church and State embodied • Its character at headquarters, in Italy • Its political character stripped of its religious cloak

CHAPTER IX: 50

Evidence enough of conspiracy adduced to create great alarm • The cause of liberty universally demands that we should awake to a sense of danger • An attack is made which is to try the *moral strength* of the republic • The mode of defense that might be consistently recommended by Austrian Popery • A mode now in actual operation in Europe • Contrary to the entire spirit of American Protestantism • True mode of defense • Popery must be opposed by antagonist institutions • Ignorance must be dispelled • Popular ignorance of all Papal countries • Popery the natural enemy of *general* education • Popish efforts to spread education in the United States delusive

CHAPTER X: 56

All classes of citizens interested in resisting the efforts of Popery • The unnatural alliance of Popery and Democracy exposed • *Religious liberty* in danger • Specially in the keeping of the Christian community • They must rally for its defense • The secular press has no sympathy with them in this struggle, it is opposed to them • The *political* character of Popery ever to be kept in mind, and opposed • It is for the Papist, not the Protestant, to separate his religious from his political creed • Papists ought to be required publicly, and formally, and officially to renounce *foreign allegiance*, and anti-republican customs

CHAPTER XI: 61

The question, what is the duty of the Protestant community, considered • Shall there be an Anti-Popery Union? • The strong manifesto that might be put forth by such a union • Such a political union discarded as impolitic and degrading to a Protestant community • Golden opportunity for showing the *moral energy* of the Republic • The lawful, efficient weapons of this contest • To be used without delay

Contents

Chapter XII: 68
  The *political* duty of *American citizens* at this crisis

Appendix A: 72
  Notes A–Q

Appendix B: 102
  The mask thrown aside

Appendix C: 108
  The rules of the Leopold Foundation, the letter of Bishop Fenwick, of Ohio, to the Emperor of Austria, and Prince Metternich's answer, are appended

Preface to the Second Edition

The great and increasing attention to the subject of which these chapters treat, has given them an extensive circulation. A large edition with notes has been rapidly sold, and two editions of the numbers, as they originally appeared in the *New York Observer*, have been printed in the Valley of the Mississippi, at the expense of patriotic Associations, and distributed throughout the western country. A larger and cheaper edition is now demanded, for general distribution, by numerous citizens belonging to various religious and opposite political sects.

The author has watched with more than ordinary solicitude, the movements throughout the country, in relation to this exciting subject, and has anxiously hoped that facts would transpire, which would prove that the charge of Conspiracy against the Liberties of the United States, conducted by the agents and funds of foreign powers, was groundless.

Gladly would he make any personal sacrifice of feeling, and endure the stigma of being accounted a visionary or an alarmist, if satisfactory counter-testimony could be adduced that might safely allay the fears that have been generally excited, and which everyone must allow are at least plausibly grounded. On the contrary, he is compelled to say, that the course of events, and further investigation, have brought full confirmation to the truth of the charge.

No one who has turned his attention to the subject can fail to have observed that the Roman Catholic journals preserve a rigid *silence* on the subject of the Austrian St. Leopold Foundation, and the alleged conspiracy against our civil institutions, through the instrumentality of the Catholic religion. Would an accusation that was groundless, so seriously implicating any Protestant sect with foreign political movements, be suffered to agitate the whole country for five or six months, without producing from the sect thus accused a prompt and satisfactory explanation?

No publication of the Roman Catholics attempting to refute the charge has, to the author's knowledge, been put forth, nor has there been

Preface to the Second Edition

(with a single exception, which he will presently examine) any disclaimer of principles hostile to our free institutions.

Silence, it would seem, has been the word of command on this subject, from headquarters; and from Maine to Louisiana, throughout the Roman Catholic ranks, with that perfectness of discipline for which this despotic sect is famous, the word of command is strictly obeyed. Neither in the daily political journals under their influence (and there are many that are evidently in their interest) has there appeared anything in the way of refutation of the charge of conspiracy, except a sneer at its improbability, or a gratuitous imputation of bigotry and intolerance, against the writer.

Many who think, with the author, that there is imminent danger to our free institutions from the increase of foreign Catholics, and from their despotic organization throughout these States, are yet unwilling to believe that Austria and other foreign despotic powers can have any settled design to subvert, through the instrumentality of the Catholic religion, the Democratic institutions of the country. Had anything more than mere dissent on this charge been hazarded, the author could better strengthen any assailed point. He is not aware of any weak spot in the chain of argument, or in the evidence by which he sustains his own belief, and he therefore must have recourse to conjecture for possible objections to its general credence.

What concurrence of circumstances, aside from *confession of the plot* is sufficient to prove conspiracy?

Is not the case proved if it can be shown:

1. That there exists an *adequate motive* to conspire?
2. That there exists *ample means* wherewith to conspire?
3. That *means capable of accomplishing the object of conspiracy are actually employed by those whose interest it is* to conspire?

No one in the case before us can expect a *confession* from the conspirators; let us have recourse then to the test proposed.

1. Have Austria and the Holy Alliance an *adequate motive* for conspiring against the liberties of the United States? Can there be a stronger motive than that of *self-preservation*? So certain as this country exists in prosperity under its present democratic form of government, just so certain will its example operate on the people

of Europe, as it has for two centuries operated, and is now in an accelerated degree operating, to subvert the ancient oppressive systems of government of the old world. The strongest motive, therefore, that can influence governments as well as individuals, that of *self-preservation*, impels Austria and the other despots of Europe to seek, *by any means in their power*, the subversion of this government.

2. Have they the *means to conspire*? No one can doubt that the usual means of conspiracy, *money*, and *intriguing agents*, are perfectly at the command of those governments who can lavish their millions for the sole purpose of protecting their thrones, who keep in their pay for this vital object, standing armies, and a police of tens of thousands of spies.

3. Have they then employed, or are they *actually employing means capable of accomplishing their object* in this country? Austria, in a combination with other powers, called the St. Leopold Foundation, has sent, and is still sending both *money* and *agents* to this country; the *former* comes in the shape of religious contributions to this St. Leopold Foundation, the Society in Vienna, established with *express reference to operations in the United States*; the *latter* come from the same quarter, in the shape of hundreds of Jesuits and priests; a class of men notorious for their intrigue and political arts, and who have a complete military organization through the United States. The Catholic religion is the cloak which covers the design.

All the circumstances, therefore, necessary to prove conspiracy, concur in fixing this charge upon Austria, and her associates in that *Union of Christian Princes*, combined in the *St. Leopold Foundation*. Is there any defect in the test I have applied, or in its application? Will it be said, that by this rule the United States can be proved to have politically conspired against India; because Protestant American Missionaries have been sent to India, to convert the people to Christianity?

Let us apply the test, and see if conspiracy can be proved.

Aside from the fact that the United States as a government cannot, as do other governments, engage in a religious enterprise, the peculiarity in its principles of the *separation of Church and State*, making it unconstitutional, and therefore impossible, I ask what *adequate motive* exists here for such a crusade?

Preface to the Second Edition

What have the United States to fear *politically* from India? It is scarcely necessary to answer, *nothing*. The proof fails, therefore, in the first rule, in regard to conspiracy *by* the United States.

But some may say, although we can easily perceive that the Austrian system and our own are diametrically opposed, and that it may be, therefore, in a general sense, for the interest of Austria to extinguish the liberties of this country, yet where is your proof that she has ever so far interested herself in the political character of this country, or considered the example of this government in so alarming a light, as to make it a serious object to destroy its influence on Europe? Can you prove that she has ever considered American institutions so dangerous to the existence of her own, as to authorize you to use so strong terms as *self-preservation*, in relation to the degree of interest she has in the event expected, and *conspiracy* in relation to measures she is using, in this country? These are important points, and I will examine them. As to the use of the term *self-preservation*, it might be a sufficient justification to refer generally to the Austrian policy, in regard to all countries, over, and in which she can exercise any control. Her interference in Saxony, to control the press, on the principle of self-preservation, is a case in point; but her interference at this moment to resist the progress of democratic opinions in Switzerland on the same principle, fully proves that she is sensibly alive to every movement in the political world which tends in the slightest degree to weaken the structure of her arbitrary system.

As to the other term, *conspiracy*, if any still think it too strong in relation to the operations of Austria in this country, I trust their opinion will be changed by considering the following facts:

In the year 1828, the celebrated Frederick Schlegel, one of the most distinguished literary men of Europe, delivered lectures at Vienna, on the Philosophy of History (which have not been translated into English), a great object of which is to show the *mutual support which Popery* and *Monarchy* derive from each other. He commends the two systems in connection, as deserving of universal reception. He attempts to prove that sciences, and arts, and all the pursuits of man as an intellectual being, are best promoted under this perfect system of church and state; a Pope at the head of the former; an Emperor at the head of the latter. He contrasts with this, the system of Protestantism; represents Protestantism as the enemy of good government, as the ally of Republicanism, as the parent of the distresses of Europe, as the cause of all the disorders with which legitimate governments are afflicted. In the close of lecture 17th, vol. ii. p. 286, he thus speaks of this country:

> "The TRUE NURSERY of all these destructive principles, the REVOLUTIONARY SCHOOL for France and the rest of Europe, has been NORTH AMERICA. Thence the evil has spread over many other lands, either by natural contagion, or by arbitrary communication."

Let it be remembered that it was in *Vienna*, in 1828, where opinions so flattering to the pride of legitimacy were publicly preached by one of the first scholars of the age, where the United States was held up to the execration of his Austrian auditors as the *"nursery of destructive principles,"* as the *"revolutionary school for Europe,"* as, in truth, the great central fire which threatened the rest of the world, and which must be put out, ere European governments could rest in safety.

Let it then also be borne in mind that it was in Vienna, in 1829, immediately after these opinions were promulgated, while the influence of Schlegel's eloquent appeals was still fresh, that the *St. Leopold Foundation* was set on foot for the purpose [to use the language of its own reports] *"of promoting the greater activity of Catholic missions in the United States."*

Here, then, we have doctrines advanced in Austria, that *Monarchy* and *Popery* mutually sustain each other, that *Republicanism* and *Protestantism* also mutually sustain each other, and that the great nursery of this hated Republicanism is these United States; and immediately consequent on the promulgation of these opinions, a great Society is formed, with the Emperor of Austria for its patron, the counsellor of State, Prince Metternich, its grand manager, and all the officers of State the zealous promoters of the design, and engaged in the instant vigorous diffusion of Popery in this country.

Now what is the intention of Austria in spreading in this country Popery, the natural ally of Monarchical government?

With the facts of the case before them, the people will not be slow in forming their judgment of the nature of this ostensibly religious enterprise, and whether the term *conspiracy* is too strong to apply to this insidious attempt.

But who, after all, is Frederick Schlegel? He may be a great scholar, but what is his situation that so much weight is to be attached to his

Preface to the Second Edition

opinions? I will give my readers a brief account of him, abridged from the *Encyclopedia Americana* (edited by a German), sufficient to enable them to judge if too much stress is laid upon his opinions:—

> "Frederick Schlegel (one of the great literary stars of Germany) went over to the Catholic faith, at Cologne, and in the year 1800 repaired to Vienna. In 1809, he received an appointment at the headquarters of the Archduke Charles, where he drew up several powerful proclamations. When peace was concluded, he again delivered lectures in Vienna on modern history and the literature of all nations. In 1812, he published the German Museum, *and gained the confidence* of Prince Metternich by various diplomatic papers, in consequence of which he was appointed Austrian counsellor of legation at the Diet in Frankfort. In 1818, he returned to Vienna, where he lived as SECRETARY OF THE COURT, and COUNSELLOR OF LEGATION, and published a view of the *Present Political Relations* [of Austria] and his complete works."

In 1828, he delivered his lectures on the Philosophy of History, in which his views as I have stated them are fully developed.

This is the man whose opinions on the relation of *Popery* and *Monarchy*, and of *Protestantism* and *Republicanism*, and of the influence of the United States, have been followed by the action of the Austrians, in the formation of the St. Leopold Foundation. *He was part and parcel of the government, he was* ONE OF THE AUSTRIAN CABINET, THE CONFIDENTIAL COUNSELLOR OF PRINCE METTERNICH!

Let me now examine matters nearer home.

How far are the Roman Catholics of this country to be considered as implicated in this Conspiracy? This is indeed a grave question, and one which demands serious attention, lest we should be, on the one hand, too regardless of danger from them, and on the other, unjust to those who are innocent.

We are told that they disclaim hostility to our free government, that they profess the warmest friendship to our democratic institutions. I readily concede that there has been, and are now, many true patriots among this sect, many estimable men of sound political views, sincere in supporting the democratic institutions of the country; but making the most ample allowance, they are but exceptions to the rule.

The sect, as a sect, is still justly chargeable with the tendency of its acknowledged principles. *If a Roman Catholic in the United States is a Democratic Republican, he is so in spite of, and in opposition to, the system of his church, and not in accordance with it.*

To the truth of this fact, the arguments of Schlegel, a Catholic, and the profoundest investigator of the subject in the present age, are unanswerably conclusive. From their principles of *passive obedience*, and the denial of the *right of private judgment* alone, Roman Catholics, as a sect, must be ignorant and willing slaves to the schemes of any despotic ecclesiastic that a *foreign power* may see fit to send to this country to rule over them. The secret plans, the real designs of the Jesuits may be confined to few bosoms, it is by no means necessary that the mass of the sect should have any knowledge of the plot; for from the nature of their system they may be blind instruments of the few.

Popery and despotism are notoriously united in the Austrian government, and Protestantism and Republicanism in that of the United States. At the time I adduced arguments to prove the truth of these two categories, I was wholly unapprised that so distinguished a political writer as Schlegel had taken the same views of these opposite systems, to rouse Austrians to the defense of their own category.

A powerful argument is derived from this corroboration of an important political truth, by Schlegel, who writes in the interest of absolutism, to urge all true friends of liberty on this side of the water, to the vigorous maintenance of the American category. It is a truth now no longer to be questioned, that Popery is so naturally the ally of Absolute government, that the diffusion of the former will result in producing the latter; and it is equally true, that the diffusion of Protestantism will result in the production of liberal institutions.

What, then, is the duty of Americans, all who really love their own free system of government?

There can be but one answer. They must unite in giving every facility to the spread of Protestant principles. Patriotism demands that every Protestant religious sect be encouraged to promote its own views, each according to the dictates of conscience; and patriotism equally demands the *discouragement*, in every lawful way, of the further introduction of Popery and Popish influence into the country.

Preface to the Second Edition

Popery is the *antagonist* to our *free system*. No one can doubt that the unusual efforts of despotic foreign governments to spread Popery in the United States, has for its principal design the subversion of our republican institutions.

Ought a vaunted but *spurious charity* to be allowed to blind the eyes of Americans to the evidence of the attack made upon them? Ought they to aid these foreign conspirators, by adding their own contributions to the means of spreading Popery? Ought they to encourage the schools of Jesuit agents; their immoral nunnery systems; their slave-making seminaries, by placing American children within the pale of their discipline? Ought they to court Jesuit influence in our politics, and screen their political principles from examination, on the plea that this is merely a *religious controversy*?

Let patriotism answer these questions.

I will now examine the *disclaimer* of hostility to our republican institutions (to which I have alluded), made in behalf of the Catholics in this country, by a Catholic journal. As a Unitarian paper in Boston has quoted it with satisfaction, I give it here, with the Unitarian editor's remarks prefixed:—

> Catholic Disclaimer.
> "We have no doubt that the Roman Catholics have their due share of proselyting spirit. Some of our good people, clergy and laity, would have a poor opinion of their sincerity if they were destitute of that spirit. But the cry is, 'Conspiracy against the Liberties of the United States.' Let the following confession of political faith pass for what it is worth. There is nothing in it which sounds like what we call by the odious epithet *Jesuitical*; and we do not ourselves question the sincerity of the avowal with which it closes; an avowal similar to one which Catholics in England have made on like occasions."—*Christian Register.*
>
> "It was the duty of the Catholic Church to perform the funeral offices for the latest representative (Carroll) of those who signed the charter of our liberties, and struggled to raise them, on their present basis of equal rights for all. The same republican opinions which he held, the Catholics of this country now hold. They deem the constitution as sacred, and the laws as obligatory in the spirit and in the

letter, as any portion of this public; and were an effort now made to consolidate religious with national government, though they should be the ruling party, as Americans, as freemen, they would be found first in the ranks to oppose such an alliance."—*Catholic Telegraph [Cincinnati]*.

This is the *disclaimer*, the only one I have yet seen, and which seems so far satisfactory to the Editor of the Register, that he sees nothing in it which "sounds Jesuitical."

To me, Jesuitism was never more evident. It is permitted to scrutinize with more than common care, a Jesuit document; but in the present case there needs no scrutiny. The trick is so on the surface, that I am surprised at the blindness of anyone who professes not to see it.

"The same republican opinions which he (Carroll) held, the Catholics of this country *now* hold," and "were an effort *now* made to consolidate religious with national government," &c.

What is there in this disclaimer which could be brought in proof of breach of faith, or even of inconsistency, if *tomorrow*, or *at any future period*, the Roman Catholics should think it politic to hold, that *"a system of government"* (like the United States) *"may be very fine in theory; very fit for imitation on the part of those who seek the power of the mob, in contradistinction to justice and the public interest; but it is not of a nature to invite the reflecting part of the world, and shows, at least, that it has evils?"*

It was *politic*, be it remarked, but yesterday (before this subject had created so much excitement), for *this same Catholic Telegraph* to hold *this identical* anti-republican, anti-American language, with the addition of his opinion, that *"the system of American Institutions was condemned by numerous other proofs."*

Today, however, the Catholic leaders find it politic to play *republican*; because the people are waking to a sense of danger to their liberties, and the artifices of the Jesuits through the land are no longer regarded with indifference.

A disclaimer on the part of the Roman Catholics, of hostility to republican institutions, is a matter of too serious importance, just now, to be left to be inferred from ambiguous expressions; it must come in a more formal and responsible shape, than that of a paragraph in a journal, of such contradictory views.

A disclaimer of anti-republican principles, of principles in direct and dangerous opposition to those of this government, with which the Papal system is directly and distinctly charged, must be a frank, unambiguous manifesto, that will bear scrutiny, issuing from an authority unquestioned. It must embrace a disclaimer of *foreign allegiance*, of *hostility to freedom of the press*, to *liberty of opinion*, to *liberty of conscience*. It must contain satisfactory evidence that these anti-American principles are expunged, and expunged forever, from the Roman Catholic system.

These are some of the essential points to be met, and they must be met without evasion. And until this is done, the people of this country are fairly borne out in regarding Roman Catholics essentially and necessarily, *enemies to her free government*, and most especially to the democratic republican institutions of this country; nor will they be blinded to this truth by the representation industriously pressed upon them, that the Catholic population of this country are *now* (whether truly or feignedly, it matters not) in favor of republican institutions, or that the foreigners among them are *now* heard more vociferous than native citizens, in their huzzas, on all patriotic occasions, and in praises of civil and religious liberty.

The course of many of our daily journals, on this subject, is one demanding severe reprehension from the American people. They are conspicuously busy in making the impression, that the excitement now general through the country respecting Popery, is the result of a sudden disposition to persecute the Catholics; that it is a sectarian and prescriptive war upon them, the fruits of an intolerant, bigoted, fanatical spirit, and the revival of ancient prejudices. These are accusations daily reiterated.

We have fallen on strange times, indeed, when subjects of the deepest political importance to the country may not be mooted in the political journals of the day without meeting the indiscriminating hostility and denunciations of such journals; without hints and even threats of popular vengeance, unless we abstain from discussing exciting subjects; as if all great questions touching our liberties could be otherwise than exciting. One would have *all debating societies suppressed*, even by mobs. Others liberally charge illiberality, bigotry, and intolerance on all who venture publicly to write against Popery, and little conscious of their own sins of the same character, are bigoted against bigotry, and intolerant against intolerance.

Denunciations like these, be it remarked, are made against any and all

Protestant sects, while Popery claims with them an exclusive privilege of exemption from attack.

Protestant American Christianity all over the land may be gratuitously charged with the local sins of an irreligious, intemperate mob, as at Charlestown; American citizens may be subjected to the grossest indignity by Roman Catholics for not conforming to Popish customs, as at Cincinnati; they may be threatened with the vengeance of a band of foreigners, as by the Superior of the Ursuline convent; they may be disturbed at religious meetings, and forcibly driven into the streets by Roman Catholic rioters, as in New York; or prevented from peaceably assembling to discuss the political question of Popery, by threats of outrage, as at Philadelphia; and in these cases, where are the sympathies of the press? Does it raise the cry of illiberality, and intolerance, and persecution, and bigotry against the Roman Catholic aggressors; does it defend the sacred right of *freedom of discussion* thus alarmingly invaded?

No! Its terms of reproach are exclusively reserved for those who venture to publish these acts. These are epithets suited only to those Protestants who have the hardihood to maintain that American necks are not yet prepared to wear the Popish yoke, the despotic chain offered by Austria, and commended to them by the royal devotees of "the blessed St. Leopold."

But, say some, this is a *religious* controversy, and it is wrong to discuss it in the daily journals. Is Popery a religious controversy? Let us see.

The St. Leopold Foundation is asserted to be a political combination of foreign powers, founded with a view to the overthrow of our republican government.

If despotism approaches us in the garb of religion, is it the less to be resisted? Have we no political interest in the truth or falsity of this fact? Is this a *religious* or a *political* question?

The agents of this society are asserted to be political agents sent to this country in the disguise of religious missionaries. Is this a *religious* or a *political* question?

The present Pope asserts his claim to temporal, as well as spiritual jurisdiction over his subjects; this jurisdiction he now exercises in other countries. Are not the Catholics of this country the subjects of the Pope; do they not owe him an allegiance superior to any due to our laws? And is this a *religious* or a *political* question?

Schools are establishing in all parts of the country, colleges, convents, and seminaries, by means of Austrian money in the hands of Jesuits. In these schools a system of education is devised altogether different from our own school system. What is the nature of this foreign system? Is it favorable or adverse to liberty? And are these *religious* or *political* questions?

Foreign emigrants are flocking to our shores in increased numbers, two thirds at least are Roman Catholics, and of the most ignorant classes, and thus pauperism and crime are alarmingly increased. The Irish Catholics in an especial manner clan together, keep themselves distinct from the American family, exercise the political privileges granted to them by our hospitality, not as Americans, but as Irishmen, keep alive their foreign feelings, their foreign associations, habits, and manners.

Is this mixture and these doings favorable or unfavorable to American character, and national independence? And is this a *religious* or a *political* question?

It would be easy to add to this list of questions purely *political*, which are involved in the mixed system of Popery; and are editors who cry out against the Popish controversy so ill-informed of the character of this *Church and State* sect, that they are unable to distinguish the *political* from the *religious* questions.

Has Popery so cloaked itself in sacredness, has this political engine of foreign despotism so sanctified its very name, that our press is awe-struck at its movements, and cries sacrilege if its political claims to our reception be in the slightest degree disputed?

Whence come all the sorrows and regrets about controversy, and lamentations and whinings about intolerance, because freemen are jealous of the meddling of foreigners in our concerns? Is this discussion of the political principles of Popery really ill-timed and gratuitous? Who has provoked it?

What! Shall foreign powers combine together, secretly and openly send their money and their agents, to spread a great political and religious system over the country; a system notorious for enslaving, impoverishing, and degrading the people; shall they build their means of attack within our borders, and American freemen be rebuked into silence, when they venture to examine the character of this foreign enterprise, and to question the purely benevolent nature of their imperial majesties' love for our souls?

It is a subject of deep interest indeed, to the community, to know how far our press is inoculated with this *no-controversy* spirit; this truly *papal* spirit; this emphatically *anti-American* spirit.

How is it that our free principles of government have been brought out, and set before the world, but by free, unembarrassed discussion; by controversy, by sharp controversy, by the collision of intellect with intellect? It is in the skillful conflict of mind with mind, that truth is elicited; it is by the friction of keen debate, that the rust of error is kept from gathering over, and corroding away vital truths. Better, far better, occasionally to endure even the excesses of the storm, so necessary to scatter the noxious vapors of the atmosphere, than to purchase a fatal repose by dwelling in the quiet but pestilential atmosphere of a tomb.

Is it the spirit of liberty or of despotism that now frowns upon free inquiry, that would shut out debate from the secular press, by the deceptive cry of *religious* controversy? Who are they that are dreading and shrinking from examination? Who that caution all those over whom they have power, "against attending upon, or taking part in, or noticing meetings," for the discussion of the political question of Popery? Ah! Is this the tender point? Is it when the *political* question is proposed for public debate, that Popish Bishops, *first* take the alarm, and the *spiritual jurisdiction* is paraded forth, and the *spiritual power* exercised, to prevent their subjects from exercising their *political* privileges? [1]

May the religious question (that alone with which Bishops have anything to do) be freely debated, without their interference. And is it only when the *political* question is started, with which as *Bishops* they have nothing *to do*, that they fulminate their spiritual thunders against those who agitate the subject? And is it in such intermeddling with politics, that they are upheld by the Protestant press? Is our press indeed in awe of Popish bishops? Does it fear to touch the civil character of Popery, for fear of giving offence to Popish bishops?

[1] Both Bishop Fenwick of *Philadelphia*, and Bishop Dubois of *New York*, have just issued orders, in *ecclesiastical* form, to those under their *jurisdiction!* to refrain from attending on the discussions where Popery is the subject of debate. These documents are worthy of notice. They will illustrate several despotic principles inherent in the Popish system: How would these orders be read by any Protestant sect, as coming from their own clergy?

Truth has nothing to fear from the severest scrutiny. It is error that loves mystery; that seeks concealment; that shrouds itself in secrecy, and cries out persecution! Yes, *persecution*, forsooth, if anyone attempts to drag it

Preface to the Second Edition

into the light. It was error that the poet aptly describes as:

>—seeing one in mail,
>Armed to point, sought back to turn again;
>For light she hated as the deadly bale,
>Aye, wont in desert darkness to remain,
>Where plain, none might her see, nor she see any plain.

This is a matter not to be covered up by silence. The political press has a fearful responsibility now resting upon it; it has a sacred duty to the country to perform, from which it cannot, must not shrink. It should be known, that there is a wider desire for knowledge on Popery, in its multifarious bearings upon society, than some seem to be aware of, and especially in its effect upon our civil institutions; a desire, which, having been created by the necessity of the times *(by the fact of unusual efforts made by foreign governments, hostile to our institutions, to spread throughout the country, Popery),* must be satisfied.

The political character of Popery is a legitimate subject of discussion in the secular press, and we believe that when the intelligent conductors of our journals shall have justly apprehended that part of the mixed system of Popery which belongs to it as a *political system*, they will no longer be deterred by the senseless cry of *religious controversy*, from lending their columns and their pens for its fearless discussion. They will see that the religious question of Popery is a separate affair, and with the discrimination that should belong to them in their responsible situations, will be able to keep the distinct religious and political character of the controversy, each within its respective limits.

The public mind is awake far and wide to the fact that Popery is a *political* as well as a religious system, nor will freemen be lulled to sleep by the Popish anodyne of *no controversy*; they will not rest till these more than suspicious maneuverings of Jesuit intriguers; of Austrian conspirators against their liberties, shall have been searched to the bottom.

Prefatory Remarks

Publisher's note: Adagio Press has re-designed this original book, with light editing for clarity and a new cover.

Our aim is to enlighten readers about the machinations of the Society of Jesus, the Jesuits, who, as you shall discover, invested much time, effort, money and blood to infiltrate the United States of America, seed her with a subservient Catholic mob, and control her from within.

This story was first reported by Samuel F.B. Morse, the inventor of the Morse code, in the early 1830s using the pseudonym Brutus, because he feared for his life and that of his family and immediate friends and colleagues. Mr. Morse knew all too well that the Jesuits would murder him, should they learn of his authorship of such a damning book. Ultimately, when the Jesuits learned of the pending publishing of Mr. Morse's book, they suppressed publication in every major city and town in America. It is perhaps a miracle the book survived at all.

Mr. Morse spent several years in Europe, mostly near Rome, observing the actions of the Jesuits and their followers, and learning of and discussing the Jesuits' intrigues with many dignitaries and other knowledgable people. Sadly, much of his discoveries were known only to those outside of America's borders, and he sought to remedy this.

What you will read in these pages will ring many a bell, as the same Jesuit intrigues of the early 1830s are still being played out today in all aspects of American society and also well beyond our own borders. When you discover this fact, we hope you will be stimulated to research the subject further.

Please consult our books on Jesuit machinations in America:

Who Really Owns Your Gold, Third Ed. by William Garner.

Romanic Depression: How the Jesuits Designed, Built and Destroyed America, Book One by Sean Maclaren.

The Suppressed Truth About the Assassination of Abraham Lincoln by Burke McCarty.

The Escape and Suicide of John Wilkes Booth: The Jesuit Assassin of

Prefatory Remarks

Abraham Lincoln by Finis L. Bates.

Fifty Years in the Church of Rome by Rev. Charles Chiniquy.

Rome's Responsibility for the Assassination of Abraham Lincoln: How the Jesuits Murdered America's Beloved President by Thomas M. Harris.

Each book also features many excellent references for further inquiry.

✝

Author's original Prefatory Remarks: The following Numbers, written for the *New York Observer* in the beginning of the year 1834, and during several weeks of confinement by indisposition, have been, perhaps, more extensively copied into the religious journals of the different Christian denominations, than any communications (with, perhaps, a single exception) of the same extent, since the establishment of religious newspapers; and although the subject matter is almost altogether *political*, giving proofs of a serious foreign conspiracy against the government, yet the writer is not aware that a single *secular* journal in the United States has taken the pains to investigate the matter, or even to ask if indeed there may not be good grounds for believing it true.

The silence of the secular press on a subject which has roused the attention of so large a body of the Protestant community, may indeed be accounted for in part, perhaps altogether, from the all-engrossing election contests which have agitated the country from one extremity of the land to the other; for the writer would certainly be very reluctant to adopt the belief which has repeatedly been urged upon him by many, that the secular journals *dare not attack Popery*; he will not believe that *dare not* ever stood in the way of the duty of any patriotic, independent conductor of the American press.[2]

At the solicitation of many citizens, without distinction of religious denomination or of political party, the writer has consented to collect the numbers into a pamphlet, adding notes illustrative of many matters which could not so well have been introduced into the columns of a newspaper.

That a vigorous and unexampled effort is making by the despotic governments of Europe to cause Popery to overspread this country, is a

[2] A friend, to whom this part was read, smiled, and said, "You are sufficiently guarded in your language, but how many *patriotic, independent* conductors of the American press are there? Can you name one?"

fact too palpable to be contradicted. Did not official documents lately published put this fact beyond dispute, yet the writer had personal evidence sufficient to convince him of the fact, and of the *political object* of the enterprise, while residing in Italy in the years 1830-31, from conversations with nobles and gentlemen of different countries, with the officers of various foreign governments, visiting and resident in the Roman and Austrian states, and with priests and other ecclesiastics of the Roman faith.

Sometimes it was hinted to him as a check to too sanguine anticipations of the triumph of the experiment of our democratic republican government; sometimes it was told him by the former class, in a tone of exultation, that a cause was in operation which would surely overthrow our institutions and gradually bring us under a form of government less obnoxious to the pride, and less dangerous to the existence of the antiquated despotic systems of Europe. In addition to these hints to the writer concerning the efforts making by the governments of Europe to carry Popery through all our borders, other American travelers will testify to similar hints made to them.

By one, I am permitted to say, that the celebrated naturalist, the late Baron Cuvier, known also as a zealous Protestant, inquired of him with marks of concern, if it were indeed true that Popery had made such progress in the United States as to cause the exultation (which, it seems, was no secret) among the legitimates of Europe.

And again, that a distinguished member of one of the Protestant German embassies in Rome also made similar inquiries of him, having heard much boasting of the progress of Popery in the United States, adding this pertinent remark,—*"they will be hammer or nails, sir; they will persecute or be persecuted."*

These facts may be of so much importance in aid of the other proofs of a conspiracy which these numbers unfold, as to show that among the various higher classes of Europe the enterprise of a Popish crusade in this country is not only a subject of notoriety, but is viewed with great interest, and is considered as having a most important *political* bearing.

In the following numbers, the writer has chosen to rest the evidence of conspiracy mainly on official documents published in Vienna, because they have been translated and published,[3] and are

[3] In the *New York Observer*, of the months of January and February, 1834.

within the reach of any citizen of the country who chooses more closely to examine them. He has also availed himself of facts in the operations of Popish agents in this country, so far as their workings have been occasionally revealed.

The writer will add in conclusion, that he writes not in the interest of a sect or a party, for the question of Popery is not identified with either political party. He has lived too long in foreign countries to be able to identify himself with the local interests of mere party at home, whether in religion or politics.

The great *democratic* features of his country's institutions, as contradistinguished from the despotic, monarchical, and aristocratic systems of Europe, were admired by him as they appeared more boldly relieved, viewed from abroad in such striking contrast to all around him; and he is thoroughly persuaded that these democratic institutions, if suffered to have their unobstructed course, unobstructed except by the natural checks of education and religion, actively and universally diffused and sustained, are more favorable to civil liberty and to the final triumph of truth, and consequently to human happiness, than any other civil institutions in the world.

The writer entertaining these views, has deemed it an imperative duty, at any sacrifice, to warn his countrymen of a subtle enemy to the democracy of the country, and to conjure them, as they value their civil and religious institutions, to watch the Protean shapes of Popery, to suspect and fear it most when it allies itself to our interests in the guise of a friend. *Mistrust of all that Popery does, or affects to do, whether as a friend or foe, in any part of the country, is the only feeling that true charity, universal charity, allows us to indulge.*

NEW YORK, January, 1835.

I

The first impression of the improbability of foreign conspiracy considered • Present political condition of Europe favors an enterprise against our institutions • The war of opinions commenced • Despotism against Liberty • The vicissitudes of this war • The official declaration of the despotic party against all liberty • Necessity to the triumph of despotism, that American liberty should be destroyed • The kind of attack upon us most likely to be adopted from the nature of the contest • Particular reasons why our institutions are obnoxious to the European governments • Has the attack commenced? Yes! By Austria, through a Society called the *St. Leopold Foundation* • Ostensibly religious in its designs

Does this heading seem singular? What, it will be said, is it at all probable that any nation, or combination of nations, can entertain designs against us, a people so peaceable, and at the same time so distant? Knowing the daily increasing resources of this country in all the means of defense against foreign aggression, how absurd in the nations abroad to dream of a conquest on this soil!

Let me, nevertheless, ask attention, while I humbly offer my reasons for believing that a conspiracy exists, that its plans are already in operation, and that we are attacked in a vulnerable quarter, which cannot be defended by our ships, our forts, or our armies.

Who among us is not aware that a mighty struggle of *opinion* is in our days agitating all the nations of Europe; that there is a war going on between *despotism* on one side, and *liberty* on the other (SEE NOTE A IN APPENDIX A). And with what deep anxiety should Americans watch the vicissitudes of the conflict!

Having long since achieved our own victory in the great strife between arbitrary power and freedom; having demonstrated, by successful experiment before the world, the safety, the happiness, the superior excellence of a republican government, a government proceeding from the people as the true source of power; enjoying in overflowing abundance the rich blessings of such a government, must we not regard with more than common interest the efforts of mighty nations to break away from the prejudices and habits, and sophistical opinions of ages of darkness, and struggling to attain the same glorious privileges of rational freedom?

But there are other motives than that of curiosity, or of mere sympathy with foreign trouble, that should arouse our solicitude in the fearful crisis which has at length arrived, a crisis which the prophetic tongue of a great British statesman (Mr. Canning) long since foretold, the *war of opinion*, threatening the world with a more frightful sacrifice of human life than history in any of its bloodstained pages records. Happily separated by an ocean-barrier from the great arena where the physical action of this bloody drama is to be performed, we are secure from the immediate physical effects of the strife; but we cannot remain unaffected by the result.

Of European wars arising from the cravings of personal ambition, from thirst for national glory, from desire of territorial increase, or from other local causes, we might safely be ignorant both of cause and result. No armed bands of a conqueror flushed with victory could give us a moment's alarm. But in a war of opinions, in a war of principles, in which the very foundations of government are subverted, and the whole social fabric upturned, we cannot, if we would, be uninterested in the result.

Principles are not bounded by geographical limits. Oceans present to them no barriers. All of principle that belongs to despotism throughout the world, whether in the iron systems of Russia and Austria, or the scarcely less civilized system of China, and all of principle that belongs to pure American freedom in the United States, or in the mixed systems of Britain, France, and some other European states, are in this great contest arrayed in opposition. The triumph of the one or the other principle, whether in the field of battle, or in the secret councils of the cabinet, or the congress of ministers, or the open debate, produces effects wherever society exists.

The recent convulsions in Europe should not pass unheeded by Americans. The three days' revolution of France; the reform in Britain on the side of liberty; the suppressed revolutions of Italy and Poland on the side of despotism; the yet doubtful victory of the two principles now in contest in Portugal and Spain[4]; the crooked diplomacy, the contradictory measures, the faithless promises of the despotic cabinets, all show that the war of principles has indeed commenced, and that Europe is agitated to its very center with the anxieties of the contest.

[4] These numbers were written in January and February, 1834.

No open annual message reveals frankly to all the world the true internal condition of the oppressed nations of Europe. From the well-guarded walls of the secret council-chamber of the imperial power, documents seldom escape to show us the strength of the opposing *principle*. Despotism glosses over all its oppressions. The people are always happy under the paternal sway. They that plead for liberty are always enemies of public order.

"Order reigns in Warsaw," was the proclamation that told the world that despotism had triumphed over Poland, and none now may know the number of her sons of freedom still at large, still unexiled to the mines of Siberia: yet it is great; for Russia, and Prussia, and Austria have leagued anew against unconquerable Poland; and the agony of determination, the desperate resolution which the Russian Autocrat has just uttered, tells the secret of the yet unvanquished spirit of Polish patriots, and at the same time discloses the plot of *mighty efforts*, of *united efforts*, of *persevering efforts*, utterly to extinguish liberty.

"As long as I live," says the Emperor, "I will oppose a will of iron to the progress of liberal opinions. The present generation is lost, but we must labor with zeal and earnestness to improve the spirit of that to come. It may require a hundred years; I am not unreasonable, I give you a whole age, but you must work without relaxation."

This is language without ambiguity, bold, undisguised; it is the clear and official disclosure of the determination of the Holy Alliance against liberty. It proclaims inextinguishable hatred, a *will of iron*. There is no compromise with liberty; a hundred years of efforts unrelaxed, if necessary, shall be put forth to crush it forever. Its very name must be blotted from the earth.

What! And is there a Holy Alliance, a *"union of Christian princes"* leagued to extinguish the kindling sparks of liberty in Europe? And will they make no effort to quench the great altar-fires that blaze in their strength in the temples of this land of liberty? An oversight like this would seem to be too palpable for the wisdom of the despotic cabinets to commit. This conquest must be achieved, or liberty will never die in Europe.

With declarations before us, thus officially put forth by despotism, of such exterminating hostility to liberty, is it not possible that an attack on us may be made from a quarter and in a shape little expected? Should we not at least look about us?

Nations may be attacked, and conquered too, with other weapons than the sword. The diplomatic pen, as England can testify, has often wrested from her that territory which her sword had won. We need not look, therefore, to the ports of Europe to see if fleets are gathering. We are safe enough from ships. Nor need we fear diplomacy, for we have "entangling alliances with none."

Where, then, shall we look? What shape would attack be likely to assume? Let the nature of the contest aid us in the inquiry. It is the war of opinion; the war of antagonist principles; the war of despotism against liberty. But how can this contest be carried on in this country? We have not the warring opinions to set in array against each other. One principle is certainly absent. We have no party in favor of despotism. This party is to be created. If then a scheme can be devised for sowing the seeds and rearing the plants of despotism, that is the scheme which would find favor with the Holy Alliance, to subserve its designs against American liberty.

It is asked: Why should the Holy Alliance feel interested in the destruction of transatlantic liberty?

I answer: The silent but powerful and increasing influence of our institutions on Europe, is reason enough.

The example alone of prosperity, which we exhibit in such strong contrast to the enslaved, priest-ridden, tax-burdened despotisms of the old world, is sufficient to keep those countries in perpetual agitation. How can it be otherwise? Will a sick man, long despairing of cure, learn that there is a remedy for him, and not desire to procure it? Will one born to think a dungeon his natural home, learn through his grated bars that man may be free, and not struggle to obtain his liberty?

I: The First Impression

And what do the people of Europe behold in this country? They witness the successful experiment of a free government; a government of the *people*; without rulers *de jure divino* (by divine right), having no hereditary privileged classes; a government, exhibiting good order and obedience to law, without an armed police and secret tribunals; a government out of debt.

They witness a people industrious, enterprising, thriving in all their interests; without monopolies; a people religious without an establishment; moral and honest without the terrors of the confessional or the inquisition; a people not harmed by the uncontrolled liberty of the press and freedom of opinion; a people that read what they please, and think, and judge, and act for themselves; a people enjoying the most unbounded security of person and property; among whom domestic conspiracies are unknown; where the poor and rich have equal justice; a people social and hospitable, exerting all their energies in schemes of public and private benefit, without other control than mutual forbearance.

A government so contrasted in all points with absolute governments, must, and does engage the intense solicitude both of the rulers and people of the old world.

Every revolution that has occurred in Europe for the last half century has been, in a greater or less degree, the consequence of our own glorious revolution. The great political truths there promulgated to the world, are the seed of the disorders, and conspiracies, and revolutions of Europe, from the first French revolution down to the present time. These revolutions are the throes of the internal life, breaking the bands of darkness with which superstition and despotism have hitherto bound the nations, struggling into the light of a new age. Can despotism know all this, and not feel it necessary to do something to counteract the evil?

Let us look around us. Is despotism doing anything in this country? It becomes us to be jealous. We have cause to expect an attack, and that it will be of a kind suited to the character of the contest, the war of opinion.

Yes! Despotism is doing something. *Austria is now acting in this country.* She has devised a grand scheme. She has organized a great plan for doing something here, which she, at least, deems important.

She has her Jesuit missionaries traveling through the land; she has supplied them with money, and has furnished a fountain for a regular supply.

[5] From the best authority, I have just learned (Dec. 1834) that $100,000 have been received from Austria within two years!

She had expended a year ago more than $74,000 in furtherance of her design!^[5]

These are not surmises. They are facts. Some *official documents*, giving the constitution and doings of this *Foreign Society*, have lately made their appearance in the *New York Observer*, and have been copied extensively into other journals of the country. This society having ostensibly a *religious* object, has been for nearly four years at work in the United States, without attracting, out of the religious world, much attention to its operations.

The great patron of this *apparently religious* scheme is no less a personage than the *Emperor of Austria*. The Society is called the *St. Leopold Foundation*. It is organized in Austria. The field of its operations is these United States. It meets and forms its plans in Vienna. Prince Metternich has it under his watchful care. The Pope has given it his apostolic benediction, and "His Royal Highness, Ferdinand V. King of Hungary, and Crown Prince of the other hereditary states, has been most graciously pleased, prompted by a piety worthy the exalted title of an apostolic king, to accept the office of Protector of the Leopold Foundation."

Now in the present state of the war of principles in Europe, is not a society formed *avowedly to act* upon this country, originating in the dominions of a despot, and holding its secret councils in his capital, calculated to excite suspicion?

Is it credible that a society got up under the auspices of the Austrian government, under the superintendence of its chief officers of state, supplying with funds a numerous body of Jesuit emissaries who are organizing themselves in all our borders, actively passing and re-passing between Europe and America; is it credible, I say, that such a society has for its object purely a *religious reform*? Is it credible that the manufacturers of chains for binding liberty in Europe, have suddenly become benevolently concerned only for the *religious welfare* of this republican people?

If this Society be solely for the propagation of the Catholic faith, one would think that *Rome*, and not *Vienna*, should be its headquarters! That the *Pope*, not the *Emperor of Austria*, should be its grand patron! It must be allowed that this should be a subject of general and absorbing interest.

If despotism has devised a scheme for operating against its antagonist principle in this country, the stronghold, the very citadel of freedom,

I: The First Impression

it becomes us to look about us. It is high time that we awake to the apprehension of danger. I propose to show why I believe this ostensibly religious society covers other designs than religious.

✝

 Political character of the Austrian government, the power attacking us • The old avowed enemy of Protestant liberty • Character of the *people* of Austria • Slaves • Character of Prince Metternich, the arch-contriver of plans to stifle liberty • These enemies of all liberty suddenly anxious for the *civil and religious liberty* of the United States • The absurdity of their ostensible design exposed • The avowed objects of Austria in the *Leopold* Foundation • Popery the instrument to act upon our institutions

THE documents to which I have alluded, exhibit so much of the correspondence of the *St. Leopold Foundation*, as it was deemed advisable to publish in Vienna. They consist of letters and statements from Jesuits, bishops and priests, residing or itinerating in this country, and whose resources are chiefly derived from the Society in Austria.

In documents thus prepared by Jesuits (the most wary order of ecclesiastics), to draw forth more liberal supplies from abroad, and then submitted to the revision of the most cautious cabinet of Europe, that so much, only may be published as will attain their object in the Austrian dominions, while all that might excite suspicion in the United States is concealed, we must expect to find great care to avoid any unnecessary exposure of covert political designs.

II: Political Character of Austrian Government

The evidence therefore of a concerted political attack upon our institutions, which I conceive to lurk under the sudden and extraordinary zeal of Austria for the *religious* welfare of the United States, will not depend altogether on the information derived from these documents. Such an attack is what might be expected from the present political attitude of the European nations, in regard to the principles of despotism and liberty, from the powerful and unavoidable effect which our institutions exert in favor of the popular principle; and also from the known political character of Austria.

Who, and what is Austria, the government that is so benevolently concerned for our religious welfare?

Austria is one of that Holy Alliance of despotic governments, one of the "union of Christian princes," leagued against the liberties of the people of Europe. Austria is one of the partitioners of Poland; the enslaver and despot of Italy. Her government is the most thorough military despotism in the world. She is the declared and consistent enemy of civil and religious liberty, of the freedom of the press; in short, of every great principle in those free institutions which it is our glory and privilege to inherit from our fathers.

Austria, from the commencement of the Reformation to the present time, has been the bitter enemy of Protestantism. The famous thirty years' war, marked by every kind of brutal excess, was waged to extirpate those very principles of civil and religious liberty which lie at the foundation of our government; and had Austria then triumphed, this republic would never have been founded.

And what are the people of Austria? They are slaves, slaves in body and mind, whipped and disciplined by priests to have no opinions of their own, and taught to consider their Emperor their God. They are the jest and byword of the Northern Germans, who never speak of Austrians but with a sneer, and "as slaves unworthy the name of Germans; as slaves both mentally and physically." [Dwight]

And who is Prince Metternich, whose letter of approval, in the name of his master the Emperor, is among the documents? He is the master of his Master, the arch-contriver of the plans for stifling liberty in Europe and throughout the world.

"Metternich," says Dwight, in his *Travels in Germany*, "by his wonderful talent in exciting fear, has thus far controlled the cabinets of Europe, and has exerted an influence over the destinies of nations, little, if any inferior to that of Napoleon." He persuaded the Emperor of Austria and King of Prussia *not to fulfill the promise* they so solemnly made to their German subjects, of giving them free constitutions.

It was the influence of Metternich that prevented Alexander from assisting Greece in her struggles for liberty. He lent Austrian vessels to assist the Turks in the subjugation of the Greeks. Metternich crushed the liberties of Spain by inducing Louis XVIII against his wishes, to send 100,000 men thither under the Duke d'Angouleme to *restore public order!* When Sicily, Naples, and Genoa, in 1820-1, threw off the galling yoke of slavery, Metternich sent his 30,000 Austrian bayonets into Italy, and re-established despotism.

And when in 1831 (as the writer can testify from personal observation), goaded to desperation by the extortion, and tyranny, and bad faith of the Papal government, the Italian patriots made a noble and successful effort to remedy their political evils by a revolution firm, yet temperate, founded in the most tolerant principles, marked by no excess, and hailed by the legations with universal joy, again did this archenemy of human happiness let loose his myrmidons, overwhelming the cities, dragging the patriots, Italy's first citizens, to the scaffold, or incarcerating them in the dungeons of Venice, filling whole provinces with mourning, and bringing back upon the wretchedly oppressed population the midnight darkness which the dawn of liberty had begun to dispel.

"Prince Metternich," says Dwight, "is regarded by the liberals of Europe as *the greatest enemy of the human race* who has lived for ages. You rarely hear his name mentioned without exciting indignation, not only in the speaker but in the auditors, Metternich has not been attacking MEN but PRINCIPLES, and has done so much towards destroying on the continent those great political truths which nations have acquired through ages of effort and suffering, that there is reason to fear, should his system' continue for half a century, liberty will forsake the continent to revisit it no more. The Saxons literally abhor this Prince.

"The German word *mitternacht* means midnight. From the resemblance of the word to Metternich, as well as from his efforts to cover Europe with political darkness, the Saxons call him Prince *Mitternacht*—Prince Midnight."

This is the government and the people which have all at once manifested so deep an interest in the *spiritual* condition of this *heretic* land. It is this nation of slaves, this remnant of the superstition, and vassalage, and

II: Political Character of Austrian Government

degradation of the dark ages, from whom the light of the nineteenth century has been so carefully shut out, that it fondly conceits its own *darkness* to be *light*, its *death-like torpor, order*—it is this nation, not yet disenthralled from the chains of superstition, that is anxious to enlighten us, in the United States, in the principles of *civil and religious liberty*. *Civil and religious liberty!* Words that may not be uttered in Austria but at the risk of the dungeon; words that would carry such shrieks of dismay through the ranks of Prince Metternich's vassals, as the flash of a torch would bring forth from a cavern of owls.

And can it be believed that such a government, the determined, consistent enemy of liberty, has no interested motive, no political design, no other than sentiments of Christian benevolence in her operations in this country?

Is it likely that we, Protestant republicans of the United States, have won the kind regards of the Austrian Government, which has been the persevering foe of the Reformation and its republican fruits since the days of Luther?

Has not Austria had vexation, and anxiety, and trouble enough for fifty years past, in stopping up the opening crevices of the European dungeon through which the unwelcome light of American liberty has so often broken, to be perfectly apprised of the hated source of that light?

Yes, she cannot but now perceive that those Protestant principles which she has been incessantly engaged in endeavoring to suppress, driven by the winds of persecution from Europe, have been taking root, and strengthening in a congenial soil, and are here bearing their genuine fruits, *liberty* and *happiness*, and all the *religious and social virtues*. She cannot view this Protestant nation growing to gigantic dimensions, a living proof of the truth and salutary influence of the principles she hates, without feeling that her own principles of darkness are in danger.

And well may she be dismayed. Yes, Austria has turned her eyes towards us, and she loves us as the owl loves the sun. Can anyone doubt that she would extinguish every spark of liberty in this country if she had the power? Can anyone believe that she would make no attempt to abate an evil which daily threatens more and more the very existence of her throne?

We may be told by some, perhaps, that her designs are purely of a religious *character*. Who can believe it? No one who has been in Austria. Every intelligent man who has resided even for a short time in the

Austrian dominions, must have seen enough of the craft, both of the government and the priests, to make him suspicious of all their doings, and most so, when they are most lavish of their professions of kindness and benevolence. *Timeo Danaos et dona ferentes.* [Beware of Greeks bearing gifts.]

But let us see what Austria avows as her design in the formation of the Leopold Foundation.[6]

The first great object is "to promote the greater activity of Catholic missions in America." She may be, and doubtless is, perfectly sincere in this design, for it is only necessary that she should succeed in her avowed object to have her utmost wishes accomplished.

She need avow no other aim. If she gains this, she gains all. If she succeeds in fastening upon us the chains of Papal bondage, she has a people as fit for any yoke she pleases to grace our necks withal, as any slaves over whom she now holds her despotic rod. She has selected a fitting instrument for her purpose. Her armies can avail her nothing against us, for the ocean intervenes. Her diplomacy gives her no hold, for there are scarcely any political relations between us. The only instrument by which she can gain the least influence in these States, is that precisely which she has chosen.

Its perfect fitness to accomplish any political design against the liberties of this country and of the world, I shall next consider.

[6] Some may be inclined to ask, is not this society a *private* association, merely chartered by the government, not differing materially from the religious societies in our own country? I answer that, were the Leopold Foundation an association of private individuals (which it is not), yet got up in the Austrian dominions, it would still be a *government affair*. For we must not confound the practices of two governments, so totally opposite in the administration of all their affairs as the Austrian and our own. From the happy separation of church and state in our own country, religious societies, of whatever character, have no connection with the government. They move in a separate sphere of action, yet in perfect harmony with it. But in Austria, no plan, no society of any kind is *private*; the government interferes in everything, is all in all. Even the persecuted Maroncelli, confined in the dungeons of Spielberg for the crime of loving the political principles of this country, must wait a week, at the risk of his life, for a gracious permission from the Paternal government *to have his leg amputated.* Yes, a private matter like this is a government affair; how much more then a grand society, with the Emperor its patron, the crown prince and heir to the imperial throne its protector, and Prince Metternich, and all the dignitaries of the empire, temporal and ecclesiastical, engaged in its operations? It is the Austrian government that is engaged in this plan of an ostensibly religious character.

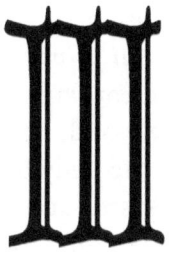

III

Popery, in its *political*, not its *religious* character, the object of the present examination • The fitness of the instrument to accomplish the political designs of despotism considered • The principles of a *despotic* and *free* government briefly contrasted • Despotic principles fundamental in Popery • Proved by infallible testimony • Papal claims of *divine right* and *plenitude of power* • Abject principles of Popery illustrated from the Russian catechism • Protestantism from its birth in favor of liberty • Luther on the 4th of July attacked the presumptuous claim of divine right • Despotism and Popery hand in hand against the liberty of conscience, liberty of opinion, and liberty of the press • The anti-republican declarations of the present Pope Gregory XVI.

Before commencing the examination of the perfect fitness of the instrument, *Catholic missions*, to accomplish the political designs, upon this country, of Austria and her despotic allies, I would premise, that I have nothing to do in these remarks with the *purely religious* character of the tenets of the Roman Catholic sect. They are not in discussion.

If any wish to resolve their doubts in the religions controversy, the acute pens of the polemic writers of the day will furnish them abundant means of deciding for themselves.

But every religious sect has certain principles of government growing out of its particular religious belief, and which will be found to agree or disagree with the principles of any given form of civil government (See Note B in Appendix A).

It is my design, therefore, briefly to consider some of the antagonist principles of the government of Austria and of the United States, and compare them with the principles of government of the Catholic and Protestant sects. By this method we shall be able to judge of their bearing on the permanency of our present civil institutions.

Let us first present to view the *fundamental principle of government*, that principle which, according to its agreement with one or the other of the two opposite opinions that divide the world, decides entirely the character of the government in every part of the body politic.

From whom is authority to govern derived? Austria and the United States will agree in answering—*from God.* The opposition of opinion occurs in the answers to the next question.

To whom on earth is this authority delegated?

Austria answers, *To the* EMPEROR, *who is the source of all authority,* "I, the EMPEROR, *do ordain,"* &c. The United States answers, *To the* PEOPLE, *in whom resides the sovereign power,* "We, the People, do ordain, establish, grant,"&c.

In one principle is recognized the necessity of the *servitude of the people*, the absolute dependence of the subject, unqualified submission to the commands of the rulers without question or examination. The *Ruler* is *Master*, the *People* are *Slaves*. In the other is recognized the *supremacy of the people*, the equality of rights and powers of the citizen, submission alone to laws emanating from themselves; the Ruler is a public servant, receiving wages from the people to perform services agreeable to their pleasure; amenable in all things to them, and holding office at their will. The *Ruler* is *Servant*, the *People* are *Master*.

The fact and important nature of the difference in these antagonist doctrines, leading, as is perceived, to diametrically opposite results, are all that is needful to state in order to proceed at once to the inquiry. Which position does the Catholic sect and the Protestant sects severally favor?

The *Pope*, the supreme Head of the Catholic church, claims to be the *"Vicegerent of God,"* "supreme over all mortals;" "over all Emperors, Kings, Princes, Potentates, and People;" "King of kings and Lord of lords." He styles himself, "the divinely appointed dispenser of *spiritual* and *temporal* punishments;" "armed with power to depose Emperors and Kings, and absolve subjects from their oath of allegiance;" "from him lies no appeal;" "he is responsible to no one on earth;" "he is judged of no one but God."

But not to go back to former ages to prove the fact of the Pope's claiming divine right, let the present Pontiff Gregory XVI testify. He claims, and attempts the exercise of this *plenitude of power*, and asserts his *divine right*.

The document I quote is fresh from the Vatican, scarce four months old, a document in which the Pope interferes directly in the political affairs of Portugal against Don Pedro. "How can there be unity in the body," says the Pope, "when the members are not united to the head, and do not obey it? And how can this union and obedience be maintained in a country where they drive from their sees the bishops, legitimately instituted by *Him* to whom it appertains to assign pastors to all the vacant churches, because the DIVINE RIGHT *grants to Him alone the primacy of jurisdiction and the plenitude of power."*

The Catholic catechism now taught by Catholic priests to the Poles in all the schools of Poland, and published by special order at Wilna, 1832, is very conclusive of the character of Catholic doctrine. The following questions and answers are propounded:—

> QUEST. 1. How is the authority of the Emperor to be considered in reference to the spirit of Christianity?
> ANS. As proceeding immediately from God.
>
> QUEST. 2. How is this substantiated by the nature of things?
> ANS. It is by the will of God that men live in society; hence the various relations which constitute society, which for its more complete security is divided into parts called nations; the government of which is entrusted to a Prince, King, or Emperor, or in other words, to a supreme ruler; we see, then, that as man exists in conformity to the will of God, society emanates from the same divine will, and more especially the supreme power and authority of our lord and master, the Czar.
>
> QUEST. 3. What duties does religion teach us, the humble subjects of his Majesty the Emperor of Russia, to practice towards him?
> ANS. Worship, obedience, fidelity, the payment of taxes, service, love and prayer, the whole being comprised in the words worship and fidelity.

QUEST. 4. Wherein does this worship consist, and how should it be manifested?
ANS. By the most unqualified reverence in words, gestures, demeanor, thoughts, and actions.

QUEST. 5. What kind of obedience do we owe him?
ANS. An entire, passive, and unbounded obedience in every point of view.

QUEST. 6. In what consists the fidelity we owe to the Emperor?
ANS. In executing his commands most rigorously, without examination, in performing the duties he requires from us, and in doing everything willingly without murmuring.

* * *

QUEST. 8. Is the service of his Majesty the Emperor obligatory on us?
ANS. Absolutely so; we should, if required, sacrifice ourselves in compliance with his will, both in a civil and military capacity, and in whatever manner he deems expedient.

QUEST. 9. What benevolent sentiments and love are due to the Emperor?
ANS. We should manifest our good will and affection, according to our station, in endeavoring to promote the prosperity of our native land, Russia, (not Poland,) as well as that of the Emperor, our father, and of his august family.

* * *

QUEST. 13. Does religion forbid us to rebel, and overthrow the government of the Emperor?
ANS. We are interdicted from so doing, at all times, and under any circumstances.

QUEST. 14. Independently of the worship we owe to the Emperor, are we called upon to respect the public authorities emanating from him?
ANS. Yes; because they emanate from him, represent him, and act as his substitute, so that the Emperor is everywhere.

III: Popery's Political Character

Quest. 15. What motives have we to fulfill the duties above enumerated?
Ans. The motives are two-fold—some natural, others revealed.

Quest. 16. What are the natural motives?
Ans. Besides the motives adduced, there are the following: The Emperor, being the head of the nation, the father of all his subjects who constitute one and the same country, is thereby alone worthy of reverence, gratitude, and obedience; for both public welfare and individual security depend on submissiveness to his commands.

Quest. 17. What are the supernatural revealed motives for this worship?
Ans. The supernatural revealed motives are, that the Emperor is the vicegerent and minister of God to execute the divine commands; and consequently, disobedience to the Emperor is identified with disobedience to God himself; that God will reward us in the world to come for the worship and obedience we render the Emperor, and punish us severely to all eternity, should we disobey and neglect to worship him. Moreover, God commands us to love and obey, from the inmost recesses of the heart, every authority, and particularly the Emperor, not from worldly considerations, but from apprehension of the final judgment.

* * *

Quest. 19. What examples confirm this doctrine?
Ans. The example of Jesus Christ himself, who lived and died in allegiance to the Emperor of Rome, and respectfully submitted to the judgment which condemned him to death. We have, moreover, the example of the Apostles, who both loved and respected them; they suffered meekly in dungeons, conformably to the will of Emperors, and did not revolt like malefactors and traitors. We must, therefore, in imitation of these examples, suffer and be silent.

This is the slavish doctrine taught to the Catholics of Poland. The people, instead of having power or rights, are, according to this catechism, mere passive slaves, born for their masters; taught, by a perversion of the threatenings of religion, to obey without murmuring, or questioning, or examination, the mandates of their human deity; bid to cringe, and fawn, and kiss the very feet of majesty, and deem themselves happy to be whipped, to be kicked, or to die in his service.

Is it necessary to say that there is not a Protestant sect in this country that holds such abject sentiments, or whose creed inculcates such barefaced idolatry of a human being?

Protestantism, on the contrary, at its birth, while yet bound with many of the shackles of Popery, attacked, in its earliest lispings of freedom, this very doctrine of *divine right*. It was Luther, and by a singular coincidence of day too, on the *4th of July*, who first, in a public disputation at Leipzig with his Popish antagonist, called in question the *divine right* of the Pope.

Let us now examine in contrast other political rights—*liberty of conscience*, *liberty of opinion*, and *liberty of the press*.

Austria and the United States differ on these points as widely as on the fundamental question. Austria not only has the press in her own territory under censorship, but intermeddles to control the press in the neighboring states on the principle of self-preservation.

"In Saxony," says Dwight, "the press is fettered by Austria and Prussia, who alleged this reason, 'that all the works published in Saxony, which are not on the *proscribed list*, are freely admitted into our dominions. *For our happiness, therefore, and the stability of our thrones, it is necessary that the press should be fettered!*'"

As to *liberty of opinion*, political or religious, in Austria, no one dreams of the existence of such a thing; the dungeon is a summary mode thereof obtaining a most happy uniformity of opinion throughout all the imperial dominions.

It is our glory, on the contrary, that all these rights are secured to us by our institutions, and freely enjoyed, not only without the least danger to the peace of the state, but from the very genius of our government, they are esteemed among its most precious safeguards.

What are the Catholic tenets on these points?

Shall I go back some three or four hundred years, and quote the pontifical law, which says [Art. 9], "The Pope has the power to interpret Scripture and to teach as he pleases, and *no person is allowed to teach in a different way*"? Or to the fourth Council of Lateran in 1215, which decrees "That all heretics (that is, all who have an opinion of their own) shall be delivered over to the civil magistrates *to be burned*"? Or shall I refer to the Catholic *Index Expurgatorius* to the list of forbidden books, to show how the press is still fettered?

No! It is unnecessary to go farther than the present day. The reigning pontiff, Gregory XVI, shall again answer the question. He has most opportunely furnished us with the present sentiments of the Catholic church on these very points. In his encyclical letter, dated Sept. 1832, the Pope, lamenting the disorders and infidelity of the times, says:

> "From this polluted fountain of 'indifference' flows that absurd and erroneous doctrine, or rather raving, in favor and defense of 'liberty of conscience,' for which most pestilential error the course is opened to that entire and wild liberty of opinion which is everywhere attempting the overthrow of religious and civil institutions, and which the unblushing impudence of some has held forth as an advantage to religion. Hence *that pest, of all others most to be dreaded in a state, unbridled liberty of opinion*, licentiousness of speech, and a lust of novelty, which, according to the experience of all ages, portend the downfall of the most powerful and flourishing empires.
> "Hither tends that worst and never sufficiently to be execrated and detested LIBERTY OF THE PRESS, for the diffusion of all manner of writings, which some so loudly contend for, and so actively promote."

He complains, too, of the dissemination of unlicensed books:

> "No means must be here omitted, says *Clement XIII*, our predecessor of happy memory, in the Encyclical Letter on the proscription of bad books—*no means* must *be here omitted*, as the extremity of the case calls for all our exertions, to *exterminate the fatal pest* which spreads through so many works, *nor* can the materials of error be *otherwise destroyed than by the flames*, which consume the depraved elements of the evil."

Now all this is explicit enough, here is no ambiguity. We see clearly, from *infallible authority*, that the Catholic of the present day, wherever he may be, if he is true to the principles of his sect, cannot consistently tolerate liberty of conscience, or liberty of the press.

Is there any sect of Protestants in this country, from whose religious tenets doctrines so subversive of civil and religious liberty can be even inferred? If there be, I am ignorant of its name. The subject will be pursued in the next chapter.

✝

The cause of Popery and despotism identical • Striking difference between Popery and Protestantism as they exist in this country • American Protestantism not controlled by Foreign Protestantism • American Popery entirely under foreign control • Jesuits, the Foreign agents of Austria, bound by the strongest ties of interest to Austrian policy, not to American • Their dangerous power • unparalleled in any Protestant sect • Our free institutions opposed in their nature to the arbitrary claims of Popery • Duplicity to be expected • Political dangers to be apprehended from Roman Catholic organization • American Roman Catholic ecclesiastical matters uncontrolled by Americans or in America; managed in a foreign country, by a foreign power, for political purposes • Consequences that may easily result from such a state of things

I EXPOSED, in my last chapter, the remarkable coincidence of the tenets of Popery with the principles of despotic government, in this respect so opposite to the tenets of Protestantism; Popery, from its very nature, favoring despotism, and Protestantism, from its very nature, favoring liberty.

Is it not then perfectly natural that the Austrian government should be active in supporting Catholic missions in this country? Is it not clear that the cause of Popery is the cause of despotism?

But there is another most striking and important difference between Popery and Protestantism, in their bearing upon the liberties of the country. *No one of the Protestant sects owns any head out of this country*, or is governed in any of its concerns by any men, or set of men, in a foreign land. All ecclesiastical officers are nominated and appointed, or removed by the people of the United States. No foreign body has any such union with any sect of Protestants in the United States, as even to advise, much less to control any of its measures. Our Episcopalians appoint their own bishops without consulting the church of England; our Presbyterians are entirely independent of the church of Scotland; and our Wesleyan Methodists have no ecclesiastical connection with the disciples of Wesley in the old world. But how is it in these respects with the Catholics?

The right of appointing to all ecclesiastical offices in this country, as everywhere else, is in the Pope (now a mere creature of Austria). He claims the power, as we have seen, by *divine right*. All the bishops, and all the ecclesiastics down to the most insignificant officer in the church, are, from the genius of the system, entirely under his control. And he, of course, will appoint none to office but those who will favor the views of Austria. He will require all whom he appoints, to support the agents whom Austria is sending to this country for the accomplishment of her own purposes.

And who are these agents? *They are*, for the most part, *Jesuits*, an ecclesiastical order proverbial through the world for cunning, duplicity, and total want of moral principle; an order so skilled in all the arts of deception, that even in Catholic countries, in Italy itself, it became intolerable, and the people required its suppression. They are Jesuits in the pay and employ of a *despotic government*, who are at work on the ignorance and passions of our community; they are foreigners, who have been schooled in foreign seminaries in the doctrine of passive obedience; they are foreigners under vows of *perpetual celibacy*, and having, therefore, no deep and permanent interest in this country; they are foreigners, bound by the strong ties of *pecuniary interest* and *ambition* to the service of a foreign despot (SEE NOTE C IN APPENDIX A).

Is there no danger to our free institutions from a host commanded by such men, whose numbers are constantly increasing by the machinations and funds of Austria?

Consider, too, the power which these Jesuits and other Catholic priests possess through *the confessional*, of knowing the private characters and affairs of all the leading men in the community; the power arising from their right to prescribe the *kinds and degrees of penance*, and the power arising from the right to *refuse absolution* to those who do not comply with their commands. Suppose such powers were exercised by

IV: Cause of Popery and Despotism Identical

the ministers of any other sect, the Episcopalian, the Methodist, the Presbyterian, the Baptist, &c., what an outcry would be raised in the land! And should not the men who possess such powers be jealously watched by all lovers of liberty?

Is it possible that these Jesuits can have a sincere attachment to the principles of free institutions? Do not these principles oppose a constant barrier to their exercise of that arbitrary power, which they claim as a divine right, and which they exercise, too, in all countries where they are dominant? Can it not be perceived, that although they may find it politic for the present to conceal their anti-republican tenets, yet this concealment will be merely temporary, and is only adopted now, the better to lull suspicion? Is it not in accordance with all experience of Popish policy, that Jesuits should encroach by little and little, and persevere till they have attained the plenitude of power?

At present they have but one aim in this country, which absorbs all others, and that is, to make themselves popular. If they succeed in this, we shall then learn, when too late to remedy the evil, that Popery abandons none of its *divine rights*. The leaders of this sect are disciplined and organized, and have their adherents entirely subservient to their will. Here, then, is a regular party, a *religious sect*, ready to throw the weight of its power as circumstances may require—ready to favor any man or set of men who will engage to favor it.

And to whom do these leaders look for their instructions? Is it to a citizen, or body of citizens belonging to this country; is it to a body of men kept in check by the ever-jealous eyes of other bodies around them, and by the immediate publicity which must be given to all their doings?

No, they are men owning no law on this side of the ocean; they are the Pope and his Consistory of Cardinals, following the plans and instructions of the imperial cabinet of Austria, plans formed in the secret councils of that cabinet, instructions delivered in secret, according to the modes of despotism, to their obedient officers, and distributed through the well-disciplined ranks in this country, to be carried into effect in furtherance of any political designs the Austrian cabinet may think advantageous to its *own interests*.

And will these designs be in favor of liberty? With a party thus formed and disciplined among us, who will venture to say that our elections will not be under the control of a Metternich, and that the appointment of a President of the United States will not be virtually made in the Imperial

Cabinet of Vienna, or the Consistory of Cardinals at Rome? Will this be pronounced incredible? It will be the almost certain result of the dominion of Popery in this country.

But we need not imagine that it will always be deemed expedient to preserve the name of President, or even the elective character of our chief magistrate. How long would it take the sophistry that deludes the mind of its victim into the belief of a man's infallibility, and fixes the delusion there indelibly, binding him, soul and body, to believe against the evidence of his reason and his senses; holding him in the most abject obedience to the will of a fellow-man; how long, I say, would it take such sophistry to impose the duty of acknowledging the divine right of an emperor over the priest-conquered vassals of this country—vassals well instructed in the Russian Catechism, and prepared to worship, love and obey, as their lord and master, some scion of the House of Hapsburg—the Emperor of the United States!

✝

V

Points in our political system which favor this foreign attack • Our toleration of all religious systems • Popery opposed to all toleration • Charge of intolerance substantiated • The organization of Popery in America connected with, and strengthened by foreign organization • Without a parallel among Protestant sects • Great preponderance of Popish strength in consequence • The divisions among Protestant sects nullifies their attempts at combination • Taken advantage of by Jesuits • Popish duplicity illustrated in its opposite alliances in Europe with despotism, and in America with democracy • The laws relating to *emigration* and *naturalization* favor foreign attack • Emigrants being mostly Catholic, and in entire subjection to their priests • No remedy provided by our laws for this alarming evil

WHAT I have advanced in my previous chapters, may have convinced my readers that there is good reason for believing that the despots of Europe are attempting, by the spread of Popery in this country, to subvert its free institutions; yet many may think that there are so many counteracting causes in the constitution of our society, that this effort to bind us with the cast-off chains of the bigotry and superstition of Europe cannot meet with success. I will, therefore, in the present chapter, consider *some of the points* in our political system, of which advantage has already been taken to attack us by the wily enemies of our liberties.

It is a beautiful feature in our Constitution, that every man is left to worship God according to the dictates of his own conscience; that the church is separated from the state, and that equal protection is granted to all creeds. In thus tolerating all sects, we have admitted to equal protection not only those sects whose religious faith and practice support the principle on which the free toleration of all is founded, but also that unique, that solitary sect, the Catholic, which builds and supports its system on the destruction of all toleration.

Yes, the Catholic is permitted to work in the light of Protestant toleration, to mature his plans, and to execute his designs to extinguish that light, and destroy the hands that hold it. It is no refutation of the charge of intolerance here made against Catholics as a sect, to show that small bodies of them under peculiar circumstances, have been tolerant, or that in this country, where they have always been a small minority, they make high professions of ardent love for the republican, tolerant institutions of our government.

No one can be deceived by evidence so partial and circumscribed, while the blood of the persecuted for opinions' sake stains with the deepest tinge every page of the history of that church, aye, even while it is still wet upon the dungeon floors of Italy; while the intolerant and anti-republican principles of Popery are now weekly thundered from the Vatican, and echoed in our ears by almost every arrival from Europe (SEE NOTE D).

Let me not be charged with accusing the Catholics of the United States with intolerance. They are too small a body as yet fully to act out their principles, and their present conduct does not affect the general question in any way, unless it may be to prove *that they are not genuine and consistent Catholics.* The conduct of a small insulated body, under the restraints of the society around it, is of no weight in deciding the character of the sect, while there are nations of the same infallible faith acting out its legitimate principles uncontrolled, and producing fruits by which all may discern, without danger of mistake, the true nature of the tree.

If Popery is tolerant, let us see Italy, and Austria, and Spain, and Portugal, open their doors to the teachers of the Protestant faith; let these countries grant to *Protestant* missionaries, as freely as we grant to Catholics, leave to disseminate their doctrine through all classes in their dominions. Then may Popery speak of toleration, then may we believe that it has felt the influence of the spirit of the age, and has reformed; but then it will not be Popery, for Popery never changes; it is infallibly the same, infallibly *intolerant.*

V: Our Toleration of all Religious Systems

The conspirators against our liberties, who have been admitted from abroad through the liberality of our institutions, are now *organized* in every part of the country; they are all subordinates, standing in regular steps of slave and master, from the most abject dolt that obeys the commands of his priest, up to the great master-slave Metternich, who commands and obeys his illustrious Master, the Emperor (SEE NOTE E IN APPENDIX A). They report from one to another, like the sub-officers of an army, up to the commander-in-chief at Vienna (not the Pope, for he is but a subordinate of Austria).[7]

There is a similar organization among the Catholics of other countries, and the whole Catholic church is thus prepared to throw its weight of power and wealth into the hands of Austria, or any Holy Alliance of despots who may be persuaded to embark, for the safety of their dynasties, in the crusade against the liberties of a country which, by its simple existence in opposition to their theory of legitimate power, is working revolution and destruction to their thrones.

Now, to this dangerous conspiracy, what have we to oppose in the discipline of Protestant sects? However well organized, each according to its own manner, these different sects may be, there is not one of them that can by any possibility derive strength, through its organization, *from foreign sects of the same name*. Nor is this a matter of regret; it is right that it should be so; no nation can be truly independent where it is otherwise. Foreign influence, then, cannot find its way into the country through any of the Protestant sects, to the danger of the State. In this respect Catholics stand alone. *They are already*

[7] Lest the charge often made in these numbers should seem gratuitous of the Pope being the creature of Austria, and entirely subservient to the Imperial Cabinet, it may be as well to state that the writer was in Rome during the deliberations of the Conclave, respecting the election of the present Pontiff. It was interesting to him to hear the speculations of the Italians on the probability of this or that cardinal's election. Couriers were daily arriving from the various despotic powers, and intrigues were rife in the ante-chambers of the Quirinal palace; now it was said that Spain would carry her candidate, now Italy, and now Austria, and when Cardinal Capelani was proclaimed Pope, the universal cry, mixed, too, with low-muttered curses, was that Austria had succeeded. The new Pope had scarcely chosen his title of Gregory XVI and passed through the ceremonies of coronation, before the revolution in his states gave him the opportunity of calling in Austria to take possession of the Patrimony of St. Peter, which his own troops could not keep for an hour, and at this moment Austrian soldiers hold the Roman Legations in submission to the cabinet of Vienna. Is not the Pope a creature of Austria?

the most powerful and dangerous sect in the country, for they are not confined in their schemes and means like the other sects, to our own borders, but *they work with the minds and the funds of all despotic Europe.*

And not only are each of the Protestant sects deprived of foreign aid; they are weak collectively, in having no common bond of union among themselves, so far as political action is concerned. The mutual jealousies of the different sects have hitherto prevented this, and it is a weakness boasted of by Catholics, and of which advantage is, and ever will be taken, while the unnatural estrangement lasts.

Catholics have boasted that they can *play off* one sect against another, for in the petty controversies that divide the contending parties, the pliable conscience of the Jesuit enables him to throw the weight of his influence on either side, as his interest may be; the command of his superiors, and the alleged *good of the church* (that is, the power of the priesthood), being paramount to all other considerations.

This pliability of conscience, so advantageous in building up any system of oppression, religious or political, presents us with strangely contradictory alliances. In Europe, Popery supports the most *high-handed despotism*, lends its thunders to awe the people into the most abject obedience, and maintains, at the top of its creed, *the indissoluble union of church and state!* While in this country, where it is yet feeling its way, (oh, how consistent!) it has allied itself with the *democracy* of the land; it is loudest in its denunciations of tyranny, the tyranny of American patriots; it is first to scent out oppression, sees afar off the machinations of the native *American Protestants* to unite church and state, and puts itself forth the most zealous guardian of civil and religious liberty! With such sentinels, surely our liberties are safe; with such guardians of our rights, we may sleep on in peace!

Another weak point in our system, is our laws, *encouraging emigration*, and affording facilities to *naturalization* (SEE NOTE F IN APPENDIX A). In the early state of the country, liberality in these points was thought to be of advantage, as it promoted the cultivation of our wild lands, but the dangers which now threaten our free institutions from this source more than balance all advantages of this character.

The great body of emigrants to this country are the hard-working, mentally neglected poor of Catholic countries in Europe, who have left a land where they were enslaved, for one of freedom. However well-disposed they may be to the country which protects them, and adopts

V: Our Toleration of all Religious Systems

them as citizens, they are not fitted to act with judgment in the political affairs of their new country, like native citizens, educated from their infancy in the principles and habits of our institutions. Most of them are too ignorant to act at all for themselves, and expect to be guided wholly by others.

These others are of course their priests. Priests have ruled them at home by *divine right*; their ignorant minds cannot ordinarily be emancipated from their habitual subjection, they will not learn nor appreciate their exemption from any such usurpation of priestly power in this country, and they are implicitly at the beck of their spiritual guides. They live surrounded by freedom, yet liberty of conscience, right of private judgment, whether in religion or politics, are as effectually excluded by the priests, as if the code of Austria already ruled the land. They form a body of men whose habits of *action* (for I cannot say *thought*) are opposed to the principles of our free institutions, for, as they are not accessible to the reasonings of the press, they cannot and do not think for themselves.

Every unlettered Catholic emigrant, therefore, that comes into the country, is adding to a mass of ignorance which it will be difficult to reach by any liberal instruction; and however honest (and I have no doubt most of them are so), yet, from the nature of things, they are but obedient instruments in the hands of their more knowing leaders, to accomplish the designs of their foreign masters. Republican education, were it allowed freely to come in contact with their minds, would doubtless soon furnish a remedy for an evil for which, in the existing state of things, we have no cure. It is but to continue for a few years the sort of emigration that is now daily pouring in its thousands from Europe, and our institutions, for ought that I can see, are at the mercy of a body of foreigners, officered by foreigners, and held completely under the control of a foreign power.

We may then have reason to say that we are the dupes of our own hospitality; we have sheltered in our well provided house a needy body of strangers, who, well filled with our cheer, are encouraged, by the unaccustomed familiarity with which they are treated, first to upset the regulations of the household, and then to turn their host and his family out of doors.

†

VI

The evil from emigration further considered • Its political bearings • The influence of emigrants at the elections • This influence concentrated in the priests • The priests must be propitiated • By what means • This influence easily purchased by the demagogue • The unprincipled character of many of our politicians favor this foreign attack • Their bargain for the suffrages of this priest-led band • A church and state party • The Protestant sects obnoxious to no such bargaining • The newspaper press favors this foreign attack • From its want of independence and its timidity • An anti-republican fondness for titles favors this foreign attack • Cautious attempts of Popery to dignify its emissaries, and to accustom us to their high-sounding titles • A mistaken notion on the subject of discussing *religious* opinion in the secular journals favors this foreign attack • Political designs not to be shielded from attack because cloaked by religion

I WILL continue the consideration of some of the points in our political system, of which the foreign conspirators take advantage, in their attacks on our liberties.

We have seen that, from the nature of the case, the emigrant Catholics, generally, are shamefully illiterate, and without opinions of their own. They are, and must be, under the direction of their priests. The press, with its arguments for or against any political measure, can have no effect on minds taught only to think as the priest thinks, and to do what the priest commands.

Here is a large body of ignorant men brought into our community, who are unapproachable by any of the ordinary means of enlightening the people—a body of men who servilely obey a set of priests imported from

VI: Evil from Emigration further Considered

abroad, bound to the country by none of the usual ties, owing allegiance and service to a foreign government; depending on that government for promotion and reward, and this reward, too, depends on the manner in which they discharge the duties prescribed to them by their foreign master; which is, doubtless for the present, to confine themselves simply and wholly to increasing the number of their sect, and the influence of the Pope in this country. It is men thus officered, and of such a character, that we have placed in all respects on a level, at our elections, with the same number of native patriotic and intelligent citizens.

The Jesuits are fully aware of the advantage they derive from this circumstance. They know that a body of men admitted to citizenship, unlearned in the true nature of American liberty, exercising the elective franchise, totally uninfluenced by the ordinary methods of reasoning, but passively obedient only to the commands of their priests, must give those priests great consequence in the eyes of the leaders of political parties; they know that these leaders must esteem it very important that the priests be propitiated.

And how is a Catholic priest to be propitiated? How, but by stipulating for that which will increase his power, or the power of the church, for be it always borne in mind that they are *identical.*

The Roman church is the body of *priests and prelates*; the *laity* have only to *obey* and to *pay*, not to exercise authority. The priest must be favored in his plans of destroying Protestantism, and building up Popery. He must have money from the public treasury to endow Catholic institutions; he must be allowed to have charters for these institutions which will confer extraordinary powers upon their Jesuit trustees (SEE NOTE G IN APPENDIX A); he must be permitted quietly to break down the Protestant Sabbath, by encouraging Catholics to buy and sell on that day as on other days.

In one word, he must have all the powers and privileges which the law, or the officers appointed to administer the law, can conveniently bestow upon him. The demagogue, or the party who will promise to do most for the accomplishment of these objects, will secure all the votes which he controls.

Surely there is great danger to our present institutions from this source, and men as skillful as are the Jesuits, we may be sure will not fail to use the power thus thrown into their hands to work great mischief to the republic.

The *recklessness* and *unprincipled* character of too many of our politicians give a great advantage to these conspirators. There is a set of men in the country who will have power and office, cost what they may; men who, without a particle of true patriotism, will yet ring the changes on the glory and honor of their country, talk loud of liberty, flatter the lowest prejudices, and fawn upon the powerful and the influential men who study politics only that they may balance the chances of their own success in falling in with or opposing this or that fluctuating interest, without caring whether that interest tends to the security or the downfall of their country's institutions.

To such politicians, a body of men thus drilled by priests presents a well fitted tool. The bargain with the priest will be easily struck. "Give me office, and I will take care of the interests of your church." The effect of the bargain upon the great moral or political interests of the country will not for a moment influence the calculation.

Thus we have among us a body of men, a *religious* sect, who can exercise a direct controlling influence in the politics of the country, and can be moved together in a solid phalanx; we have a *church interfering directly and most powerfully in the affairs of state.*

There is not in the whole country a parallel to this among the other sects. What clergyman of the Methodists, or Baptists, or Episcopalians, or of any other denomination, could command the votes of the members of their several congregations, in the election of an individual to political office? The very idea of such power is preposterous to a Protestant. No freeman, no man accustomed to judge for himself, would submit even to be advised, unasked, by his minister in a matter of this kind, much less *dictated to.*

Connected with these evils, and assisting to increase them, we have a *Press* to an alarming extent *wanting in independence.*

Most of our journals are avowedly attached to a particular party, or to particular individuals. They are like counsel retained for a particular cause; they are to say everything that makes in favor of their client, and conceal everything that makes against him. Does a question of principle arise, of fundamental importance to the country? The inquiry with a journal thus pledged is not, how are our free institutions, how is the country affected by the decision, but how will the decision affect the interests of our particular party or favorite? How few are there among our newspaper editors who dare to take a manly stand for or against a principle that affects vitally the constitution, if it is found to bear unfavorably upon their party or their candidate!

A press thus wanting in magnanimity and independence is the fit instrument for advancing the purposes of unprincipled men; and editors of this stamp—and they are confined to no particular party—whether they have followed out their conduct or not to its legitimate results, can easily be made the tools of a despot, to subvert the liberties of their country.

Again; we have, still unsubdued, some weaknesses (perhaps they belong to human nature) of which advantage may be taken to the injury of our republican character, and in aid of despotism, and which may seem to some too trivial to merit notice in connection with the more serious matters just considered.

One of these weaknesses is an *anti-republican fondness for titles* (SEE NOTE H IN APPENDIX A); and whoever has lived in the old world, and knows the extraordinary and powerful influence which mere titles of honor exercise over the minds of men, and their tendency to keep in due subjection the artificial ranks into which despotic and aristocratic power divide the people, subduing the lower orders to their lords and masters, will not think it amiss in this place to draw attention to the subject.

Republicans as we are, I fear we are influenced in a greater degree than we are aware, by the high sounding epithets with which despotism and aristocracy surround their officers, to awe into reverence the ignorant multitude. A name having half a dozen titles for its *avant couriers*, and as many for its rear guard, swells into an importance even in the estimation of our citizens, which the name alone, and especially the individual himself, could never assume.

Let Mr. Brown or Mr. Smith, or any other intelligent, upright, active citizen, be elected president of a benevolent society, does he excite the gaze of those who meet him, or inspire awe in the multitude? No one regards him but as a respectable, useful member of the community.

But let us learn that a gentleman, not half as intelligent, or upright, or active, is to land in our city, who is announced as the *"Most Illustrious Archduke and Eminence, his Imperial Highness, the Cardinal and Archbishop of Olmutz,* RODOLPH (this last is the gentleman's real name), *Highest Curator of the Leopold Foundation,"* and although not half as capable in any respect as Mr. Brown or Mr. Smith, or ten thousand other honest untitled citizens among us, I very much fear that the Battery would be thronged, and the windows in Broadway would be in demand, and the streets filled with a gaping crowd, to see a man who could have such a mighty retinue of glittering epithets about him. Yet this title-blazoned gentleman holds the same office as Mr. Brown or Mr. Smith. Poor human nature! Alas for its weakness![8]

Who is not struck with the difference of effect upon the imagination when we describe a person thus: *"Mr.—, a good-hearted old gentleman, rather weak in the head, who finds in the manufacture of sealing-wax one of the chief and most agreeable employments of his time;"* and when we should describe a man thus: *"His Imperial Majesty* FRANCIS I., *Emperor of Austria, King of Jerusalem, Hungary, Bohemia, of Lombardy and Venice, Dalmatia, Croatia, Sclavonia, Galizia, and Lodomiria, Archduke of Austria, Duke of Lorena, Salzburg, Styria, Carinthia, and Carniola, Grand Prince of Transylvania, Margrave of Moravia, Count Prince of Hapsburg and Tyrol,"* &c.; and yet these two descriptions belong to one and the same individual.

[8] There is reason to believe we are reforming in this particular, for we have now tilled foreigners, respectable men, travelers in the country, and our press no longer lends itself to announce their unimportant presence or movements.

There used to be a sound democratic feeling in the country, which spurned such glosses of character, and frowned out of use *mere glory-giving title*.

Austria, however, is gradually (as fast as it is thought safe) introducing these titled gentlemen into the country. Bishop Fenwick, a Catholic priest, is *"his Grace of Cincinnati;"* Mr. Vicar-General Rese, another priest, is only *"his Reverence;"* and Bishop Flaget, and all the other Bishops, are simple *Monseigneurs*, this title in a *foreign language* being less harsh at present to republican ears than its plump aristocratic English translation, *"My Lord Bishop of New York," "My Lord Bishop of Boston," "My Lord Bishop of Charleston,"* &c.

As we improve, however, under Catholic instruction, we may come to be quite reconciled even to his Eminence, Cardinal so and so, and to all the other graduated fooleries which are so well adapted to dazzle the ignorant. The scarlet carriage of a Cardinal, too, bedizened with gold, and containing the sacred person of some Jesuit, all scarlet and humility, as is at this day often seen in Rome, may yet excite our admiration as it rolls through our streets.

Even a *Pope* (for in these republican times in Italy, who knows but his Holiness may have leave of absence)—yes, even a *Pope, a Vicegerent of God*, the great divinely appointed appointer of Rulers, the very center from which all titles emanate—may possibly, in his scarlet and gold and jewel-decked equipage, astonish our eyes, and prostrate us on our knees as he moves down Broadway. To be sure, some of his republican friends, now in strange holy alliance with his faithful subjects here, might find their Protestant knees at first a little stiff, yet the Catholic schools, which they are encouraging with their votes and their money and their influence, will soon furnish them good instructors in the art of reverential gesture and genuflection.

Again, there are some minds of a peculiarly sensitive cast, that cannot bear to have the subject of religious opinion mooted in any way in the secular journals. They use a plausible argument that satisfies them, namely, that religion is too sacred a subject to be discussed by the daily press.

I agree to a certain extent, and in a modified sense, with this sentiment; but it should be remembered that all is not *religion* which passes under that name. The public safety makes it necessary sometimes to strip off the disguise, and show the true character of a design which may have assumed the sacred cloak, the better to pass unchallenged by just such feeble-hearted objectors.

Were such objections valid, how easy would it be for the most dangerous political designs (as in the case we are considering) to assume a religious garb, and so escape detection.

The exposure I am now making of the foreign designs upon our liberties, may possibly be mistaken for an attack on the Religion of the Catholics; yet I have not meddled with the conscience of any Catholic. If he honestly believes the doctrine of *Transubstantiation*, or that by doing *penance* he will prepare himself for heaven, or in the existence of *Purgatory*, or in the efficacy of the *prayers and masses* of priests to free the souls of his relatives from its flames, or that it is right to worship *the Virgin Mary*, or to *pray to Saints*, or keep *holy days*, or to *refrain from meat* at certain times, or to *go on pilgrimages*, or in the *virtue of relics*, or that *none but Catholics can be saved*, or many other points; however wrong I may and do think him to be, it is foreign from the design of these chapters to speak against them.

But when he proclaims to the world that all power, *temporal* as well as *spiritual*, exists in the Pope (denying, of course, the fundamental doctrine of republicanism), that *liberty of conscience* is a *"raving,"* and *"most pestilential error;"* that *"he execrates and detests the liberty of the press;"*

when his intolerant creed asserts that no faith is to be kept with *heretics* (all being heretics, in the creed of a Catholic, who are not Catholics) and many other palpable *anti-republican*, as well as immoral doctrines, he has then blended with his creed *political* tenets that vitally affect the very existence of our government, and no association with *religious* belief shall shield them from observation and rebuke.

It would indeed be singular if these mere *"ravings"* (the Pope's phrase is appropriate here), subversive of the fundamental principles of our government, should be shielded from exposure because misnamed *religion*. If incendiaries or robbers should ensconce themselves within a church, from the windows and towers of which they were assailing the people, the cry of sacrilege shall not prevent us from attempts to dislodge them, though the walls which protect them should suffer in the conflict.

VII

The *political* character of this ostensibly *religious* enterprise proved from the letters of the Jesuits now in this country • Their antipathy to *private judgment* • Their anticipations of a change in our form of government • Our government declared too free for the exercise of their divine rights • Their political partialities • Their cold acknowledgment of the generosity, and liberality, and hospitality of our government • Their estimate of our condition contrasted with their estimate of that of Austria • Their acknowledged allegiance and servility to a foreign master • Their sympathies with the oppressor, and not with the oppressed • Their direct avowal of *political* intention

Let me next show the *political* character of this ostensibly *religious* effort, from the sentiments of the Austrian emissaries expressed to their foreign patrons.

The very nature of a conspiracy of this kind precludes the possibility of much *direct* evidence of political design; for Jesuit cunning and Austrian duplicity would be sure to tread with unusual caution on American ground. Yet if I can quote from their correspondence some expressions of *antipathy to our free principles and to the government; some hinting at the subversion of the government; prevailing partialities for arbitrary government; and siding with tyranny against the oppressed;* and some *acknowledgments of* POLITICAL EFFECTS *to be expected from the operations of the society*, I shall have exhibited evidence enough to put every citizen, who values his birthright, upon the strict watch of these men and their adherents, and to show the importance of some measures of repelling this insidious invasion of the country.

The Bishop of Baltimore, writing to the Austrian Society, laments the wretched state of the Catholic religion in Virginia, and as a proof of the difficulty it has to contend with (a proof doubtless shocking to the pious docility of his Austrian readers), he says:

> "I sent to Richmond a zealous missionary, a native of America. He travelled through the whole of Virginia. The Protestants flocked on all sides to hear him; they offered him their churches, court-houses, and other public buildings, to preach in—which, however, is not at all surprising, for the people are divided into numerous sects, and know not what faith to embrace. In consequence of being spoiled by bad instruction, *they will judge everything themselves*; they therefore hear eagerly every newcomer...."

The Bishop, if he had the power, would of course change this "*bad instruction,*" for better, and, as in Catholic countries, would relieve them from the trouble of *judging for themselves.*

Thus the *liberty of private judgment* and *freedom of opinion*, guaranteed by our institutions, are avowedly an obstacle to the success of the Catholics. Is it not natural that Catholics should desire to remove this obstacle out of their way?[9]

My Lord Bishop Flaget, of Bardstown, Kentucky, in a letter to his patrons abroad, has this plain hint at an *ulterior political design*, and that no less than the *entire subversion* of our *republican government.* Speaking of the

---

[9] A Catholic journal of this city (the *Register and Diary*) was put into my hands as I had completed this last paragraph. It contains the same sentiment, so illustrative of the natural abhorrence of Catholics to the exercise of private judgment, that I cannot forbear quoting it.

"We seriously advise Catholic parents to be very cautious in the choice of schoolbooks for their children. There is more danger to be apprehended in this quarter than could be conceived. Parents, we are aware, have not always the time or patience to examine these matters: *but if they trust implicitly to us, we shall, with God's help, do it for them. Legimus ne legantur."* We read, that they may not read!

How kind! They will save parents all the trouble of judging for themselves, but *"we must be trusted implicitly!"* Would a Protestant journal thus dare to take liberties with its readers?

VII: Political Character of Religious Enterprise Proved

difficulties and discouragements the Catholic missionaries have to contend with in converting the Indians, the last difficulty in the way he says, is "their continual traffic among the whites, WHICH CANNOT BE HINDERED AS LONG AS THE REPUBLICAN GOVERNMENT SHALL SUBSIST!"

What is this but saying that a republican government is unfavorable in its nature to the restrictions we deem necessary to the extension of the Catholic religion; when the time shall come that the present government shall be subverted, which we are looking forward to, or hope for, we can then hinder this traffic?

Mr. Baraga, the German missionary in Michigan, seems impressed with the same conviction of the unhappy influences of a free government upon his attempts to make converts to the church of Rome. In giving an account of the refusal of some persons to have their children baptized, he lays the fault on this "TOO FREE (allzu freien) GOVERNMENT." In a more despotic government, in Italy or Austria, he would have been able to put in force compulsory baptism on these children (SEE NOTE I IN APPENDIX A).

Those few extracts are quite sufficient to show how our form of government, which gives to the Catholics all the freedom and facilities that all other sects enjoy, does from its very nature embarrass their despotic plans.

Accustomed to dictate at home, how annoying it is to these Austrian ecclesiastics to be obliged to put off their authority; to yield their divine right of judging for others; to be compelled to get at men through their reason and conscience, instead of the more summary way of compulsion! The disposition to use force, if they could, shows itself in spite of all their caution. The inclination is there. It is reined in by circumstances. They want only strength to act out the inherent despotism of Popery.

But let me show what are some of the *political partialities* which these foreign emissaries discover in their letters and statements to their Austrian supporters.

They acknowledge their unsuspicious reception by the people of the United States; they acknowledge that Protestants in all parts of the country have even aided them with money to build their chapels, and colleges, and nunneries, and treated them with liberality and hospitality, and—strange infatuation!—have been so monstrously foolish as to entrust their children to them to be educated! So infatuated as to confide in their honor and in their promises that they would use no attempts to proselyte them!

And with all this, does it not once occur to these gentlemen, that this liberality, and generosity, and openness of character are the fruits of Protestant republicanism?

Might we not expect at least that Popery, were it republican in its nature, would find something in all this that would excite admiration, and call forth some praise of a system so contrasted to that of any other government; some acknowledgments to the government of the country that protects it, and allows its enemies the unparalleled liberty *even to plot the downfall of the state*? But no, the government of the United States is not once mentioned in praise. The very principle of the government, through which they are tolerated, is thus slightingly noticed: "The government of the United States has thought fit to adopt a complete indifference towards all religions." (*Quart. Regist.* Feb. 1830, p.198.)

They can recognize no nobler principle than indifference.

Again, of the *people* of our country they thus write: "We entreat all European Christians to unite in prayer to God for the conversion of these *unhappy heathen* and *obstinate heretics*."

We are spoken of as a country *"on which the light of faith has hitherto not shined,"* "A vast country, destitute of all spiritual and temporal resources."

But if Austria is mentioned, what are the terms?

"Your Society (the Leopold Foundation), which is an ornament to the *illustrious Austrian Empire,"*—*"the noble and generous inhabitants*" of the Austrian empire;" "Of many circumstances in our condition, few, perhaps, in your *happy empire* can form a correct notion;" and again, "Here are many churches, if you may so call the miserable wooden buildings, differing little from the barns of your happy land!" *Austria*, happy land!

How enthusiastic, too, is another Bishop, who writes, "we cannot sufficiently praise *our good Emperor* (of Austria) *were we to extol him to the third heaven!"*

Such are the *political partialities* which are discovered in various parts of these documents. Are they in favor of our republican darkness, and heathenism, and misery, or of Austrian light, and piety, and happiness?

In the struggles of the European people for their liberty, do these foreign teachers *sympathize with* the *oppressor* or with the *oppressed*?

"France no more helps us," (Charles X. had just been dethroned), "and Rome, beset by *enemies to the church and public order*, is not in a

VII: Political Character of Religous Enterprise Proved

condition to help us."

And who are these men, stigmatized as *enemies of public order?* They are the Italian patriots of the Revolution of 1831, than whom our own country, in the perils of its own revolution, did not produce men more courageous, more firm, more wise, more tolerant, more patriotic; men who had freed their country from the bonds of despotism in a struggle almost bloodless, for the people were with them; men who, in the spirit of American patriots, were organizing a free government; rectifying the abuses of Papal misrule, and who, in a few weeks of their power, had accomplished years of benefit. These are the men afterwards dragged to death, or to prison, by *Austrian intruders*, and styled by our Jesuits, *enemies of public order!* Austria herself uses the selfsame terms to stigmatize those who resist oppression.

I will notice one extract more, to which I would call the special attention of my readers. It is from one of the reports of the society in Lyons, which society had the principal management of American missions under Charles X. When this bigoted monarch was dethroned, and liberal principles reigned in France, the society so languished that Austria took the design more completely into her own hands, and through the Leopold Foundation she has the enterprise now under her more immediate guardianship.

> "Our beloved king (Charles X) has given the society his protection, and has enrolled his name as a subscriber. Our society has also made rapid progress in the neighboring states of Piedmont and Savoy. The pious rulers of those lands, and the chief ecclesiastics, have given it a friendly reception."

Charles X, be it noticed, and the despotic rulers of Piedmont and Savoy, took a special interest in this American enterprise. The report goes on to say:

> "Who can doubt that an institution which has a *purely spiritual aim*, whose only object is the conversion of souls, desires nothing less than to make whole nations, on whom the light of faith has hitherto not shined, partakers of the knowledge of the Gospel; an institution solemnly

sanctioned by the supreme head of the church: which, as we have already remarked, enjoys the protection of our pious monarch, the support of archbishops and bishops; an institution established in a city under the inspection of officers, at whose head stands the great almoner, and which numbers among its members men alike honorable for their rank in church and state; an institution of which his excellency, the minister of church affairs, lately said, in his place in the Chamber of Deputies, that, independent of its *purely spiritual design*, IT WAS OF GREAT POLITICAL INTEREST."

Observe that great pains are here taken to impress upon the public mind the *purely spiritual aim*, the *purely spiritual design* of the society; and yet one of the French ministers, in the Chambers of Deputies, states directly that it has another design, and that it was of "GREAT POLITICAL INTEREST." He gives some of these political objects: "because it planted the French name in distant countries; caused it, by the mild influence of our missionaries, to be loved and honored, and thus opened to our trade and industry useful channels," &c.

Now, if *some political effects* are already avowed, as intended to be produced by this society, and that, too, immediately after reiterating its *purely spiritual design*, why may not that *particular* political effect be also intended, of far more importance to the interests of despotism, namely, *the subversion of our Republican institutions*?

☨

VIII

Some of the means by which Jesuits can already operate *politically* in the country • By mob discipline • By *priest police* • Then great danger • Already established • Proofs • Priests already rule the mob • Nothing in the principles of Popery to prevent its interference in our elections • Popery interferes at the present day in the politics of other countries • Popery the same in our country • It interferes in our elections • In Michigan, Charleston, S.C., and New York • Popery a political despotism cloaked under the name of Religion • It is Church and State embodied • Its character at headquarters, in Italy • Its political character stripped of its religious cloak

B︎ut some of my readers, notwithstanding they may be convinced that it is for the interest of despotism to subvert our institutions, and are even persuaded that this grand enterprise has been actually undertaken, may be inclined to ask in what manner can the despots of Europe effect, by means of Popish emissaries, anything in this country to counteract the influence of our liberal institutions?

In what way can they operate here?

With the *necessity existing of doing something, from the instinct of self-preservation*, to check the influence of our free institutions on Europe, with the *funds* provided, and *agents* on the spot interested in their plans, one would think it needed but little sagacity to find modes and opportunities of operating; especially, too, when such *vulnerable points* as I have exposed (and there are many more which I have not brought forward) invite attack.

To any such inquirers, let me say there are many ways in which a body organized as are the Catholics, and moving in concert, might *disturb* (to use the mildest term) the good order of the republic, and thus compel us to present to observing Europe the spectacle of republican anarchy. Who is not aware that a great portion of that stuff which composes a mob, ripe for riot or excess of any kind, and of which we have every week or two a fresh example in some part of the country, is a Catholic[10] population? And what makes it turbulent? Ignorance—an ignorance which it is for the interest of its leaders not to enlighten; for, enlighten a man, and he will think for himself, and have some self-respect; he will understand the laws, and know his interest in obeying them. Keep him in ignorance, and he is the slave of the man who will flatter his passions and appetites, or awe him by superstitious fears.

[10] At the time this was written, riots in this country were almost entirely confined to the emigrants from foreign countries employed as laborers on our railroads, canals, &c.

Against the outbreakings of such men, society, as it is constituted on our free system, can protect itself only in one of two ways: it must either bring these men under the influence and control of a sound republican and religious education, or it must call in the aid of *the priests* who govern them, and who may *permit* and *direct*, or restrain their turbulence, in accordance with what they may judge at any particular time to be the *interest of the church*.

Yes, be it well remarked, the same hands that can, whenever it suits their interest, restrain, can also, at the proper time, "*let slip the dogs of war.*" In this mode of restraint by a *police of priests*, by substituting the *ecclesiastical* for the *civil power*, the *priestled* mobs of Portugal and Spain, and South America, are instructive examples. And start not, American reader, *this kind of police is already established in our country!* We have had mobs again and again, which neither the civil nor military power have availed anything to quell, until the magic "*peace, be still,*" of the *Catholic priest* has hushed the winds, and calmed the waves of popular tumult. (SEE NOTE J in Appendix A.)

While I write, what mean the negotiations between two Irish bands of emigrants in hostile array against each other, shedding each other's blood upon our soil, setting with the bayonet miserable foreign feuds which they have brought over the waters with them? Why have not the civil and

VIII: Means by which Jesuits already Operate Politically

military power been able to restore order among them and obedience to our laws, without calling in the *priests* to negotiate and settle the terms on which they will cease from violating our laws?[11]

Have the priests *become necessary* in our political system? Have the emissaries of a foreign despotic power stolen this march upon us? Can they tell their foreign masters, "*we already rule the mob*"? Yes, and facts will bear them out in their boasting. (SEE NOTE K in Appendix A.)

And what now prevents the interference of Catholics, as a sect, directly in the *political elections* of the country? They are organized under their priests; is there anything in their religious principles to restrain them? Do not Catholics of the present day use the bonds of religious union to effect political objects in other countries? Did not the Pope interfere in Poland in the late revolution, and, through the priests, command submission to the tyranny of the Czar?

---

[11] As our readers have probably forgotten the particulars of the affair here alluded to, we subjoin, from the *Journal of Commerce*, a copy of the agreement subscribed by the leaders of the riot. The civil and military authorities of Maryland had tried repeatedly, but in vain, to quell the rioters.—*Ed. Obs.*

From the *Journal of Commerce:*

THE RIOTERS.—It appears by the following notice, that the rioters on the Baltimore and Washington Railroad have concluded a treaty of peace, through the intervention of a priest. There was considerable talk during the late riots in this city, of calling in the agency of the priests to put an end to the disturbance. No doubt it would have been effectual.

AGREEMENT.

On the 24th of June, 1834, the subscribers, in the presence of the Rev. John McElroy, have respectively and mutually agreed to bury forever, on their own part, and on behalf of their respective sections of country, all remembrance of feuds and animosities, as well as injuries sustained. They also promise to each other, and make a sincere tender of their intention to preserve peace, harmony, and good feeling between persons of every part of their native country without distinction.

They further mutually agree to exclude from their houses and premises, all disorderly persons of every kind, and particularly habitual drunkards. They are also resolved, and do intend to apply, in all cases where it is necessary, to the civil authorities, or to the laws of the country for redress—and finally, they are determined to use their utmost endeavors to enforce, by word and example, these their unanimous resolutions.

Signed by fourteen of the men employed on the 4th, 5th, and 8th sections of the 2nd division, B. and W.R.R. (on behalf of all employed);

And also by thirteen of the 8th section of the 1st division. 5 employed (on behalf of all employed).

At the moment I am writing, are not monks and priests leaders in the field of battle in Spain, in Portugal? Is not the Pope encouraging the troops of Don Miguel, and exciting priests and people to arms in a civil contest? Has Popery abandoned its ever-busy meddling in the politics of the countries where it obtains foothold? (SEE NOTE L in Appendix A.)

Will it be said, that however officious in the old countries, yet here, by some strange metamorphosis, Popery has changed its character, and is modified by our institutions, that here it is surely religious, seeking only the religious welfare of the people, that it does not meddle with the state? (SEE NOTE M in Appendix A.)

It is not true that Popery meddles not with the politics of the country. The cloven foot has already shown itself. *Popery is organized at the elections!*

For example: in Michigan, the Bishop Richard, a Jesuit (since deceased), was several times chosen delegate to Congress from the territory, the majority of the people being Catholics. As Protestants became more numerous, the contest between the bishop and his Protestant rival was more and more close, until at length, by the increase of Protestant emigration, the latter triumphed. The bishop, in order to detect any delinquency in his flock at the polls, *had his ticket printed on colored paper!* Whether any were so mutinous as not to vote according to orders, or what penance was inflicted for disobedience, I did not learn. The fact of such a truly Jesuitical mode of espionage I have from a gentleman resident at that time in Detroit.

Is not a fact like this of some importance? Does it not show that Popery, with all its spaciousness, is the same here as elsewhere? It manifests, when it has the opportunity, its genuine disposition to use *spiritual* power for the promotion of its *temporal* ambition. It uses its ecclesiastical weapons to control an election.

In Charleston, S.C. the Roman Catholic Bishop, England, is said to have boasted of the number of votes that he could control at an election. I have been informed, on authority which cannot be doubted, that in New York, a priest, in a late election for city officers, stopped his congregation after mass on Sunday and urged the electors not to vote for a particular candidate, on the ground of his being an anti-Catholic. The result was the election of the Catholic candidate.

It is unnecessary to multiply facts of this nature, nor will it be objected that these instances are unworthy of notice, because of their local or circumscribed character. Surely American Protestants, freemen, have

VIII: Means by which Jesuits already Operate Politically

discernment enough to discover beneath them the cloven foot of this subtle foreign heresy, and will not wait for a more extensive, disastrous, and overwhelming political interference, ere they assume the attitude of watchfulness and defense. They will see that Popery is now, what it has ever been, a system of the darkest *political* intrigue and despotism, cloaking itself, to avoid attack, under the sacred name of religion. They will be deeply impressed with the truth, that Popery is a *political* as well as a religious system; that in this respect it differs totally from all other sects, from all other forms of religion in the country. *Popery embodies in itself* THE CLOSEST UNION OF CHURCH AND STATE.

Observe it at the fountainhead. In the Roman States the civil and ecclesiastical offices are blended together in the same individual. The *Pope* is the *King*. A *Cardinal* is *Secretary of State*. The *Consistory of Cardinals* is the *Cabinet Council*, the *Ministry*, and they are *Viceroys* in the provinces. The *Archbishops* are *Ambassadors* to foreign courts. The *Bishops* are *Judges* and *Magistrates*; and the road to preferment to most, if not all the great offices of state, is through the priesthood.

In Rome, and the patrimony of St. Peter, the *temporal* and *spiritual* powers are so closely united in the same individual, that no attack can be made on any *temporal* misrule without drawing down upon the assailants the vengeance of the *spiritual* power exercised by the same individual. Is the Judge corrupt or oppressive, and do the people rise against him—the *Judge* retires into the *Bishop*, and in his sacred retreat cries, "Touch not the Lord's anointed."

Can we not discern the *political* character of Popery? Shall the name of *Religion*, artfully connected with it, still blind our eyes?

Let us suppose a body of men to combine together, and claim as their right, that *all public and private property, of whatever kind, is held at their disposal;* that *they alone are to judge of their own right to dispose of it;* that they alone are authorized *to think or speak on the subject;* that *they who speak or write in opposition to them are traitors,* and must *be put to death; that all temporal power is secondary to theirs, and amenable to their superior and infallible judgment;* and the better to hide the presumption of these tyrannical claims, suppose that these men should pretend to *divine right*, and call their system *Religion*, and so claim the protection of our laws, and pleading conscience, demand to be tolerated. Would the name of *Religion* be a cloak sufficiently thick to hide such absurdity, and shield it from public indignation?

Take, then, from *Popery* its name of *Religion*; strip its *officers* of their pompous titles of *sacredness*, and its *decrees* of the nauseous cant of *piety*,[12] and what have you remaining? Is it not a *naked, odious Despotism*, depending for its strength on the observance of the strictest military discipline in its ranks, from the Pope, through his Cardinals, Archbishops, Bishops, &c. down to the lowest priest of his dominions? And is not this despotism acting *politically* in this country?

[12] Through the Leopold Foundation reports there is this perpetual cant of piety: We have "pious prelate," "pious purpose," "pious end," "pious curiosity," "pious dread," "pious progress," and even "pious dress."

Let us suppose, for the sake of illustration, that the Emperor of Russia, in a conceited dream of divine right to universal empire, should parcel out our country into convenient districts, and should proclaim his intention to exercise his rightful sway over these states, now not owning his control; should we not justly laugh at his ridiculous pretensions?

But suppose he should proceed to appoint his *Viceroys, Grand Imperial Dukes*, giving to one the title of "*his Grace of Albany*," to another the "*Grand Duke of Washington*," and to another "*his Imperial Highness of Savannah*," and should send them out to take possession of their districts, and subdue the people as fast as practicable to their proper obedience to his legitimate sway; and should these pompous Viceroys, with their train of sub-officers, actually come over from Russia, and erect their government houses, and commence by compliant manners and fair promises to procure *lands* and *rentals* to hold in the power of the Emperor, and under the guise of educating the rising generation should begin to sap the foundations of their attachment to the government, by blinding their reasoning faculties, and by the Russian catechism instilling the doctrine of passive obedience, and the *divine right of the Emperor*; what would we say to all this?

Ridiculous as the first conceited dream of imperial ambition appeared, if matters got to this pass, we should begin to think that there was something *serious* in the attempt, and, very properly too, be a little alarmed.

Suppose then, further, that the Emperor's cause, by Russian emigration, and the money supplied by the Emperor, had become so strong that the Viceroys were emboldened, in a cautious way, to try their influence upon some of the local elections; that the Russian party had become a body somewhat formidable; that its *foreign leaders* had their passive obedience

VIII: Means by which Jesuits already Operate Politically

troops so well under command as to make themselves necessary in the *police* of the country; that we feared to offend them, that the secular press favored them[13] and the *unprincipled courted them*; to what point then, in the process of gradually surrendering our liberties to the Russian Czar, should we have come; and how near to their accomplishment would be those wild dreams of imperial ambition, which we had, in the first instance, ridiculed?

And is this a caricature? What is the difference between the *real* claims, and efforts, and condition of Popery at this moment in these United States, and the *supposed* claims, and efforts, and condition of the Russian despotism? The one comes disguised under the name of *Religion*, the other, more honest and more harmless, would come in its real *political* name. Give the latter the name of *Religion*, call the Emperor, *Pope*, and his *Viceroys*, *Bishops*, interlard the *imperial* decrees with *pious cant*, and you have the case of pretension, and intrigue, and success, too, which has actually passed in these United States!

[13] Is this a harsh judgment on the secular press? If a secular paper ventures to remonstrate against Catholics, is not the cry of *intolerance* or *persecution* at once raised, and the editor scared away from his duty of exposing the secret *political* enemies of the republic, under the false notion that he is engaged in a *religious* controversy?

[14] "Indiana and Illinois, two states depending on my jurisdiction!"—My Lord Bishop Flaget's Letter.

Yes, the King of Rome, acting by the promptings of the Austrian Cabinet, and in the plentitude of his usurpation, has already extended his scepter over our land; he has divided us up into provinces, and appointed his Viceroys, who claim their *jurisdiction*[14] from a higher power than exists in this country, even from his majesty himself, who appoints them, who removes them at will, to whom they owe allegiance; for the extension of whose temporal kingdom they are exerting themselves, and whose success, let it be indelibly impressed on your minds, is the *certain destruction of the free institutions of our country.*

☩

Evidence enough of conspiracy adduced to create great alarm • The cause of liberty universally demands that we should awake to a sense of danger • An attack is made which is to try the *moral strength* of the republic • The mode of defense that might be consistently recommended by Austrian Popery • A mode now in actual operation in Europe • Contrary to the entire spirit of American Protestantism • True mode of defense • Popery must be opposed by antagonist institutions • Ignorance must be dispelled • Popular ignorance of all Papal countries • Popery the natural enemy of *general* education • Popish efforts to spread education in the United States delusive

Is not the evidence I have exhibited in my previous numbers sufficiently strong to prove to my countrymen the existence of a *foreign conspiracy* against the liberties of the country? Does the nature of the case admit of stronger evidence? Or must we wait for some positive, undisguised acts of oppression, before we will believe that we are attacked and in danger? Must we wait for a formal declaration of war?

The serpent has already commenced his coil about our limbs, and the lethargy of his poison is creeping over us; shall we be more sensible of the torpor when it has fastened upon our vitals?

The *house is on fire*; can we not believe it till the flames have touched our flesh? Is not the enemy already organized in the land? Can we not perceive all around us the evidence of his presence? Have not the wily maneuverings of despotism already commenced? Is he not inveigling our children to his schools? Is he not intriguing with the press? Is he not usurping the *police* of the country, and showing his front in our political councils?

Because no foe is on the sea, no hostile armies on our plains, may we sleep securely? Shall we watch only on the outer walls, while the sappers and miners of foreign despots are at work under our feet, and steadily advancing beneath the very citadel? Where is that unwearying vigilance which the eloquent Burke proclaimed to be the characteristic of our fathers, who did not wait to feel oppression, but *"augured misgovernment at a distance, and snuffed the approach of tyranny in every tainted breeze!"* Are we their sons, and shall we sleep on our posts?

We may sleep, but the enemy is awake; he is straining every nerve to possess himself of our fair land. We must awake, or we are lost. Foundations are attacked, fundamental principles are threatened, interests are put in jeopardy, which throw all the questions which now agitate the councils of the country into the shade.

It is *Liberty itself* that is in danger, not the liberty of a single state, no, nor of the United States, but the *liberty of the world.* Yes, it is the *world* that has its anxious eyes upon us; it is the *world* that cries to us in the agony of its struggles against despotism, the WORLD EXPECTS AMERICA, REPUBLICAN AMERICA, TO DO HER DUTY.

Our institutions have already withstood many assaults from within and from without, but the war has now assumed a new shape. An effort is now making that is to try the MORAL STRENGTH *of the Republic.* It is not a physical contest on the land or on the water. The issue depends not on the strength of our armies or navies. How then shall we defend ourselves from this *new*, this subtle attack?

"Defend yourselves!" cries the Austrian Papist; "you cannot defend yourselves; your government, in its very nature, is not strong enough to protect you against foreign or domestic conspiracy. You must here take a lesson from legitimate governments; we alone can teach the effectual method of suppressing conspiracies.

"You say you have a body of conspirators against your liberties, a body of foreigners who are spreading their pernicious heresies through your land, and endangering the state. The weakness of republicanism is now manifest. What constitutional or legal provision meets the difficulty? Where are your laws *prohibiting Catholics* from preaching or teaching their doctrines, and erecting their chapels, churches, and schools? Where is your *passport system*, to enable you to know the movements of every man of them in the land? Where is your *Gens d'armerie*, your armed police, those useful agents, whose *domiciliary visits* could ferret out every Catholic, seize and examine his papers, and keep him from further mischief in the dungeons of the state? Where are your laws that can terrify, by the penalty of imprisonment, any man that dares to utter an opinion against the government?

"Where is your *judicious censorship of the press*, to silence the Catholic journals, and stifle any Catholic sentiments in other journals? Where is your *Index Expurgatorius*, to denounce all unsafe books, that no Catholic book may be printed or admitted into the country? Where is your system of *espionage*, that no Protestant may read a Catholic publication, or express in conversation a single sentiment unfavorable to Protestantism, without being overlooked and overheard by some faithful spy, and reported to the government? Where are the officers in your post-office department for the *secret examination of letters*, so that even the most confidential correspondence may be purified from dangerous heresy? Where is your *secret Inquisitorial Court* for the trial and condemnation of apostate Protestants?

"Without these changes in the constitution and laws of your government, you can oppose no efficient obstacle to the success of this conspiracy."

And what shall I reply to this consistent Papist? The methods he would prescribe have the sanction of successful experiment for some centuries. *They are in sober truth the very means that Popery employs* at this very day, in the countries where it is dominant, to prevent the spread of opinions contrary to its own dogmas.

But are these the methods that commend themselves to American Protestants? Does not such a cumbrous machinery of chains, and bolts, and bayonets, and soldiers, to hold the mind in bondage, seem rather a dream of the dark ages, than a real system now in actual operation in the nineteenth century? Away with Austrian and Popish precedent. American Protestantism is of a different school. It needs none of the aids which are indispensable to the crumbling despotisms of Europe; no soldiers, no restrictive enactments, no *Index Expurgatorius*, no Inquisition.

This war is the war of principles; it is on the open, field of free discussion; and the victory is to be won by the exercise of moral energy,

IX: Evidence of Conspiracy Adduced

by the force of religious and political truth. But still it is a *war*, and all true patriots must wake to the cry of danger. They must up and gird themselves for battle.

It is no false alarm. Our liberties are in danger. The Philistines are upon us. Their bonds are prepared, and they intend, if they can, to fasten them upon our limbs. We must shake off our lethargy, and like the giant awaking from his sleep, snap these shackles asunder. We are attacked in vulnerable points by foreign enemies to all liberty.

We must no longer indulge a quiet complacency in our institutions, as if there were a charm in the simple name of American liberty sufficiently potent to repel all invasion. For what constitutes *the life* of our justly cherished institutions? Where is the living principle that sustains them? Is it in the air we breathe? Is it in the soil we cultivate? Is our air or our soil more congenial to liberty than the air and soil of Austria, or Italy, or Spain? No! The life of our institutions!

It is a *moral* and *intellectual* life; it lies in the culture of the human mind and heart, of the reason and conscience; it is bound up in principles which must be taught by father to son, from generation to generation, with care, with toil, with sacrifice.

Hide the Bible for fifty years—we will not ask for the hundred years so graciously granted by the autocrat to stifle liberty—hide the Bible for fifty years, and let our children be under the guidance of men whose first exercise upon the youthful mind is to teach that lesson of old school sophistry which distorts it forever, and binds it through life in bonds of error to the dictation of *a man*—a man whom, in the same exercise of distorted reason, he is persuaded to believe infallible; let these Jesuit doctors take the place of our Protestant instructors, and where will be the political institutions of the country? Fifty years would amply suffice to give the victory to the despotic principle, and realize the most sanguine wishes of the tyrants of Europe.

The first thing to be done to secure safety, is to open our eyes at once to the reality and *the extent of the danger*. We must not walk on blindly, crying "all's well." The enemy is in all our borders. He has spread himself through all the land. The ramifications of this foreign plot are everywhere visible to all who will open their eyes.

Surprising and unwelcome as is such an announcement, we must hear it and regard it. We must make AN IMMEDIATE, A VIGOROUS, A UNITED, A PERSEVERING EFFORT TO SPREAD RELIGIOUS AND INTELLECTUAL

CULTIVATION THROUGH EVERY PART OF OUR COUNTRY. Not a village nor a log-hut of the land should be overlooked. Where Popery has put darkness, we must put light. Where Popery has planted its crosses, its colleges, its churches, its chapels, its nunneries, Protestant patriotism must put side by side college for college, seminary for seminary, church for church.

And the money must not be kept back. Does Austria send her tens of thousands to subjugate us to the principles of darkness? We must send our hundreds of thousands, ay, our millions, if necessary, to redeem our children from the double bondage of spiritual and temporal slavery, and preserve to them American light and liberty.

The food of Popery is ignorance. Ignorance is the mother of Papal devotion. Ignorance is the legitimate prey of Popery.

But someone here asks, are not the Roman Catholics establishing schools and colleges, and seminaries of various kinds, in the destitute parts of the land? Are they not also zealous for education? May we not safely assist them in their endeavors to enlighten the ignorant?

Enlighten the ignorant! Does Popery enlighten the ignorant of Spain, of Portugal, of Italy, of Ireland, of South America, of Canada? What sort of instruction is that, in the latter country for example, which leaves 78,000 out of 87,000 of its grown up scholars, signers of a petition *by their mark*, unable to write their own names, and many of the remaining signers who *write nothing but their names*? What sort of light is that which generates darkness? Popery enlighten the ignorant! *Popery is the natural enemy of* GENERAL *education.*

Do you ask for proof? It is overwhelming.

Look at the intellectual condition of all the countries where Popery is dominant. If Popery is in favor of *general* education, why are the great mass of the people, in the papal countries I have named, the most ill-informed, mentally degraded beings of all the civilized world, arbitrarily shut out by law from all knowledge but that which makes them slaves to the tyranny of their oppressors? No! Look well to it!

If Popery in this country is professing friendship to general knowledge, it is a feigned alliance. If it pretends to be in favor of educating the poor, it is a false pretense, it is only *temporizing*; it is *conforming for the present, from policy*, to the spirit of Protestantism around it, that it may forge its chains with less suspicion. If it is establishing schools, it is to make them *prisons* of the youthful intellect of the country. If the Papists in Europe are really desirous of enlightening ignorant Americans by establishing schools, let them make their first efforts among their brethren of the same faith in Canada and Mexico.

Do our fellow citizens at the South and West ask for schools, and are there not funds and teachers enough in our own land of wealth and education to train up our own offspring in the free principles of our own institutions? Or are we indeed *so beggared* as to be dependent *on the charities of the Holy Alliance, and the Jesuits of Europe,* for funds and teachers to educate our youth—in what?—THE PRINCIPLES OF DESPOTISM!

Forbid it, patriotism! Forbid it, religion! Our own means are sufficient; we have wealth enough, and teachers in abundance. We have only to will it with the resolution and the zeal that have so often been shown, whenever great national or moral interests are to be subserved, and every fortress, every corps of Austrian darkness will be surrounded; the lighted torches of truth, political and religious, would flash their unwelcome beams into every secret chamber of the enemies of our liberty, and drive these ill-omened birds of a foreign nest to their native hiding-place.

☨

All classes of citizens interested in resisting the efforts of Popery • The unnatural alliance of Popery and Democracy exposed • *Religious liberty* in danger • Specially in the keeping of the Christian community • They must rally for its defense • The secular press has no sympathy with them in this struggle, it is opposed to them • The *political* character of Popery ever to be kept in mind, and opposed • It is for the Papist, not the Protestant, to separate his religious from his political creed • Papists ought to be required publicly, and formally, and officially to renounce *foreign allegiance*, and anti-republican customs

IN CONSIDERING the means of counteracting this foreign political conspiracy against our free institutions, I have said that we must awake to the *reality and extent of the danger*, and rouse ourselves to *immediate* and *vigorous action*, in spreading religious and intellectual cultivation through the land. This, indeed, would be effectual, but this remedy is remote in its operation, and is most seriously retarded by the enormous increase of ignorance which is flooding the country by *foreign emigration*. While, therefore, the remote effects of our exertions are still provided for, the pressing exigency of the case seems to require some more immediate efforts to prevent the further spread of the evil.

The *two-fold* character of the enemy who is attacking us must be well considered. Popery is doubly opposed—*civilly* and *religiously*—to all

X: Unnatural Alliance between Popery and Democracy

that is valuable in our free institutions. As a *religious* system, it is the avowed and common enemy of every other religious sect in the land. The Episcopalian, the Methodist, the Presbyterian, the Baptist, the Quaker, the Unitarian, the Jew, &c., are alike anathematized, are together *obstinate heretics*, in the creed of the Papist. He wages an indiscriminate, uncompromising, exterminating war with all.

As a political system, it is opposed to every political party in the country. Popery in its very nature is opposed to the genius of our free system, notwithstanding its affected, artful appropriation (in our country only) of the habits and phraseology of democracy. Present policy alone dictates so *unnatural* an alliance, ay, *most unnatural alliance*.

What! *Popery* and *Democracy* allied? Despotism and Liberty hand in hand? Has the Sovereign Pontiff in very deed turned Democrat in the United States? Let us look into this incongruous coalition, this solecism in politics—*Popish Democracy*.

Do Popish Bishops or Priests consult *the people*? Have *the people* any voice in ecclesiastical matters? Can *the people* vote their own taxes, or are they imposed upon them by irresponsible priests? Do the bishops and priests account for the manner in which they spend *the people's money*? Has Popery here adopted the American principle of RESPONSIBILITY TO THE PEOPLE; a responsibility which gives the most insignificant contributor of his money towards any object, a right to examine into the manner in which it is disbursed? No! *The people account to their priests in all cases, not the priests to the people in any case.* What sort of Democracy is that where *the people have no power, and the priests have all*, by divine right? Let us hear no more of the presumptuous claim of Popery to Democracy.

Popery is the antipodes of Democracy. It is the same petty tyrant of the people here, as in Europe. And this is the tyranny that hopes to escape detection, by assuming the name, and adopting the language of Democracy (SEE NOTE N in Appendix A). It is this tyranny that is courted and favored at political elections by our politicians of all parties, because it has the advantage of a despotic organization.[15]

How much longer are the feelings of the religious community to be scandalized, and their moral sense outraged, by the barefaced bargainings for Catholic and infidel votes? Have the

[15] And infidelity too, it seems, has just learned the secret of political power, and, not content with civil and religious liberty, has introduced a third kind, and organizing itself into a new interest, demands to be represented in the state as the advocate of irreligious liberty!

religious community no remedy against such outrage? If they have not, if there is not a single point on which they can act together, if the religious denominations of various names can have no understanding on matters of this kind, if they have no common bond to unite them in repelling common enemies, then let us boast no more of religious liberty.

What is *religious* liberty? Is it merely a phrase to round a period in a Fourth of July oration? Is it a dazzling sentiment for Papists to use in blinding the eyes of the people, while they rivet upon them their foreign chains of superstition? Is it a shield to be held before infidels, from behind which they may throw their poisoned shafts at all that is orderly and fair in our *civil*, as well as religious institutions?

Or is it that prize above all price, that heaven-descended gift to the world, for which, with its twin-sister, we contended in our war for independence, and which we are bound, by every duty to ourselves, to our children, to our country, to the world, to guard with the most jealous care? And has it ever occurred to Christians that this duty of guarding *religious liberty in a more special manner devolves on them!*

Who but the religious community appreciate the inestimable value of religious liberty? Are their interests safe in the hands of the infidel, who scoffs at all religion, and uses his civil liberty to subvert all liberty?

Is it safe in the hands of imported radicals and blasphemers? Is it safe in the hands of calculating, selfish, power-seeking politicians? Is it safe in the keeping of Metternich's stipendiaries, the active agents of a foreign despotic power? Does the secular press take care of our religious liberty? Is there a secular journal that has even hinted to its readers the existence of this double conspiracy?

The most dangerous politico-religious sect that ever existed; a sect that has been notorious for ages for throwing governments into confusion, is politically at work in our own country, under the immediate auspices of the most despotic power of Europe, interested politically and vitally in the destruction of our free institutions, and is any alarm manifested by the secular press?

No! They are altogether silent on this subject. They presume it is only a *religious* controversy, and they cannot meddle with religious controversies. They must not expose religious imposture, lest they should be called *pious*. They have no idea of blending church and state. They have a religion of their own, a worship in which the public, they think, feel a more exciting interest. One has a *liberty pole* to be erected, another a

X: Unnatural Alliance between Popery and Democracy

hickory tree; and the rival pretensions to superiority of these wooden gods of their idolatry it is of the last importance to settle, and the bacchanalian revelry of their consecration must be recorded and blazoned forth in italics and capitals in its minutest particulars:

"O Pole! O Tree! Thou art the preserver of our liberty!"

No; if the *religious community* (in which term I mean to include Protestants of every name who profess a religious faith) awake not to the defense of their own rights in the state, if they indulge timidity or jealousy of each other, if they will not come forward boldly and firmly to withstand the encroachments of corruption upon their own rights; the selfish politicians of the day (and they swarm in the ranks of all parties) will bargain away all that is valuable in the country, civil and religious, to the Pope, to Austria, or to any foreign power that will pay them the price of their treason.

We cannot be too often reminded of the *double* character of the enemy who has gained foothold upon our shores; for although Popery is a religious sect, and on this ground claims toleration side by side with other religious sects, yet Popery is also a *political*, a *despotic system*, which we must repel as altogether incompatible with the existence of freedom. I repeat it, Popery is a *political*, a *despotic system*, which must be resisted by all true patriots.

Is it asked, how can we separate the characters thus combined in one individual? How can we repel *the politics* of a Papist without infringing upon his *religious* right?

I answer, that this is a difficulty for Papists, not for Protestants to solve. If Papists have made their *religion* and *despotism* identical, that is not our fault. Our religion, the *Protestant religion*, and *Liberty*, are identical, and liberty keeps no terms with despotism. American Protestants use no such solecism as *religious despotism*. Shall *political heresy* be shielded from all attack, because it is connected with a *religious creed*? Let Papists separate their religious faith from their political faith, if they can, and the former shall suffer no political attack from us.

"But no," the Papist cries, "I cannot separate them; my religion is so blended with the political system, that they must be tolerated or refused together; my 'whole system is *one, and indivisible, unchangeable, infallible.*' I am conscientious, I cannot separate them." What are we to do in such a case? Are we to surrender our civil and religious liberty to such presumptuous folly?

No! *Our liberties must be preserved*; and we say, and say firmly to the Popish Bishops and Priests among us, *give us your declaration of your relation to our civil government. Renounce your foreign allegiance, your allegiance to a* FOREIGN SOVEREIGN. *Let us have your own avowal in an official manifesto, that the Democratic Government under which you here live delights you best. Put your ecclesiastical doings upon as open and popular a footing as other sects. Open your books to the people, that they may scrutinize your financial matters, that the people, your own people, may know how much they pay to priests, and how the priests expend their money; that the poorest who is taxed from his hard earned wages for church dues, and the richest who gives his gold to support your extravagant ceremonial, may equally know that their contributions are not misapplied. Come out and declare your opinion on the* LIBERTY OF THE PRESS, *on* LIBERTY OF CONSCIENCE, *and* LIBERTY OF OPINION.

Americans demand it. They are waking up. They have their eyes upon you. Think not the American Eagle is asleep. Americans are not Austrians, to be hoodwinked by Popish tricks. This is a call upon you, you will be obliged soon to regard. Nor will they be content with partial, obscure avowals of republican sentiment in your journals, by insulated priests, or even bishops. The American people will require a more serious testimonial of your opinions on these fundamental political points.

You have had *Convocations of Bishops at Baltimore*. Let us have at their next assembling, their sentiments on these vital points. Let us have *a document full and explicit, signed by their names, a document that may circulate as well in Austria and Italy as in America; ay, a document that may be published "con permissione"' in the Diario di Roma,* and be circulated to instruct the faithful in *the united church, the church of but one mind,* in the sentiments of American democratic Bishops on these American principles. *Let us see how they will accord with those of his Holiness, Pope Gregory XVI, in his late encyclical letter!*

Will Popish Bishops dare to put forth such a manifesto? No! They dare not.

XI

The question, what is the duty of the Protestant community, considered • Shall there be an Anti-Popery Union? • The strong manifesto that might be put forth by such a union • Such a political union discarded as impolitic and degrading to a Protestant community • Golden opportunity for showing the *moral energy* of the Republic • The lawful, efficient weapons of this contest • To be used without delay

THERE is no question of more pressing, more vital importance to the whole country than this: *What is the duty of the Protestant community in the perilous condition to which religious as well as civil liberty is reduced, by the attempts of Popery and foreign enemies upon our free institutions?*

Have Christian patriots reflected at all on the possible, nay, I will say probable loss of religious liberty; or in idea attempted to follow out to their result, and in their immeasurable extent, the fearful consequences of its loss? Why is it, then, that no more energetic efforts are made to save ourselves?

> ——we hear this fearful tempest sing,
> Yet seek no shelter to avoid the storm;
> We see the wind sit sore upon our sails,
> And yet we strike not, but securely perish.
>
> * * * * * * * * *
>
> We see the very wreck that we must suffer;
> And unavoided is the danger now,
> For suffering so *the causes* of our wreck.
>
> —*Shakespeare.*

Yes, the rocks are in full view on which American liberty must inevitably be wrecked, unless all hands are roused to immediate action. Our dangers are nonetheless, be assured, because they are not those against which the general cry of alarm is so loudly raised by the two great political parties of the day.

In the heedless strife they are now waging, the most superlative epithets of alarm have been already exhausted by each, on fictitious or comparatively trivial dangers to the commonwealth. The public ear is deafened by their noise; its sense of hearing is grown callous with the reiterated cries of alarm on every slight occasion. "Wolf! Wolf!" has been so often falsely cried, that now, when the wolf has in reality appeared, we cannot be made to realize it. "If the trumpet give an uncertain sound, who shall prepare himself for the battle?"

We are busying ourselves in quenching the few falling sparks that threaten the deck of the ship, without heeding the fire beneath, that is approaching the magazine.

In this reckless warfare of passion, and falsehood, and slander, and aided by the deafening din of party strife, neither party seem to have observed that a secret enemy, an artful, foreign enemy, has stolen in among us, joining his *foreign accents* to swell the uproar, that he may with less suspicion do his nefarious work (See Note O in Appendix A). Like incendiaries at a conflagration, they even *cry fire! loudest*, and are most ostentatiously busy in seeming to protect that very property which they watch but to make their prey.

What then can be done? Shall Protestants organize themselves into a political union after the manner of the Papists, and the various classes of industry and even of *foreigners* in the country? Shall they form an Anti-Popery Union, and take their places among this strange medley of conflicting interests? And why should they not? Various parties and classes do now combine and organize for their own interest; and if any class of men are allowed thus to combine and promote their own peculiar interests at the expense of another class, that other class surely has at least an equal right to combine to protect itself against the excess of its antagonist. A denial of this right would certainly come with an ill grace from those who are already formed into separate organizations, as a *Working Men's* party, as a *Trades' Union* party, as a *Catholic* party, as an *Irish* party, as a *German* party, yes, even as a *French* and an *Italian* party.[16]

And now, on the supposition that such a political organization of Protestants were expedient (for it resolves itself altogether into a question of expediency), let us see whether any party or interest could show a stronger claim upon the support of the whole nation. Its manifesto might run thus:

Popery is a *political system, despotic* in its organization, *anti-democratic* and *anti-republican*, and cannot therefore co-exist with American republicanism.

The ratio of increase of *Popery* is the exact ratio of decrease of *civil liberty*.

The *dominance of Popery* in the United States is the *certain destruction of our free institutions*.

Popery, by its organization, is wholly under the control of a FOREIGN DESPOTIC SOVEREIGN.

AUSTRIA, *one of the Holy Alliance of sovereigns* leagued against the liberties of the world, HAS THE SUPERINTENDENCE OF THE OPERATIONS OF POPERY IN THIS COUNTRY.

[16] By classing these together at this moment, I do not intend to commit myself as expressing approval or disapproval of the right of each and all of these to organize, but merely to show that such organization does already exist among other classes in the community, and if even *foreigners* among us are allowed to exercise the right to organize into a separate interest, yes, even as foreigners, can the right with any propriety be refused to American Christians? Having thus stated the case, I am now free to make the passing remark, that excluding from view the three classes first named, the right of *foreigners* to organize as *foreigners*, for political purposes, is at least very questionable; but were their right unquestionably legal through the mildness of our laws, yet the practice is dangerous, indecorous, and a palpable abuse of political liberality. The Irish naturalized citizens who should know no other name than Americans, for years have clanned together as Irish, and every means has been used, and is still used, *especially by Catholics*, to preserve them *distinct from the American family*. Recently a portion of the Germans have organized to keep up their distinct *nationality*, and the French and Italians have just followed the example. [Nov. 1834.] To what will all this lead?

The agents of Austria in the United States are Jesuits and priests in the pay of that foreign power, in active correspondence with their employers abroad, not bound by ties of any kind to our government or country, but, on the contrary, *impelled by the strongest motives of ambition* to serve the interests of a despotic foreign government; which *ambition* has already, in one or more instances, been gratified, by promotion of these agents to higher office and wealth in Europe.

Popery is a UNION OF CHURCH AND STATE, *nor can Popery exist in this country in that plenitude of power* which it claims as a divine right, and which, in the very nature of the system, it must continually strive to obtain, *until such a union is consummated*. Popery on this ground, therefore, is destructive to our *religious* as well as civil liberty.

Popery is more dangerous and more formidable than any power in the United States, on the ground that, through its despotic organization, it can *concentrate its efforts* for any purpose with complete effect; and that organization being wholly under *foreign* control, it can have no real sympathy with anything American. The *funds*, and *intellect*, and *intriguing experience of all Papal and despotic Europe*, by means of agents at this moment organized throughout our land, can, at any time, be brought in aid of the enterprises of foreign powers in this country.

These are the grounds upon which an appeal for support might be made to the patriotism, the love of liberty, the hatred of tyranny, temporal and spiritual, which belong in common to the whole Protestant American family.

But is this the plan of opposition to Popery that should be proposed, the plan which ought to be adopted by the Protestant community?

No; distinctly and decidedly no. Plausible as it may appear, and perfectly in accordance as it is with the practice of politicians, the Christian community *ought not*, *cannot* adopt such an organization. There must not be a Christian *party*.

What! Shall Christianity throw aside the keen moral and intellectual arms with which alone it has gained and secured every *substantial* victory since the commencement of its glorious career; shall it exchange those arms of heavenly temper, "mighty in pulling down strongholds," for the paltry, earthly (I might even say infernal) weapons of party strife? Can Christianity stoop so low? Can it bring itself down from contemplating its great work of revolutionizing the world, by bringing moral truth to bear on the conscience and the heart, and narrow its vision to the contracted sphere of party politics? Can it enter, without defilement, into the polluted and polluting arena of political contest? Can it consent to be bargained for by political hucksters, or have the price of its favors hawked in the market by political brokers? (See Note P in Appendix A.) Can it consent to compete with Popery in the use of those instruments of intrigue, and trick, and gambling management, in which Popery is perfectly skilled from the hoarded experience of ages? Can Christians present themselves before the country and the world, in this enlightened age and country, as a mere political party?

No, no; God forbid that we should forget the holy character of our cause; let us not be caught in that snare of the enemy. The danger-cry of *Church and State* may safely be left to the people, to trumpet aloud through the land, when the blind infatuation which now closes their eyes shall have been removed, and they shall be able to see, what many already see, the secret political maneuverings (See Note Q in Appendix A) of a sect whose very existence depends upon a union of Church and State.

No; let American Christianity proclaim anew to all the world that it can never be wooed to any such unholy alliance. It will keep its garments unspotted from the crimes of the State. It will take none of the responsibilities of the political errors of the age, nor father any of the evils which the unprincipled politicians of the day may bring upon the country and the world, as the effect of their political bargainings.

Now is the time for this Christian Republic to show her *moral* energy.

Europe is an anxious spectator of our contests, and is watching the success of this new trial of the strength of our boasted institutions. Oh! What a lesson, what an impressive lesson might free America now read to Europe! What an example of the power of *moral* over *physical* government can she give to the world, if she will but rouse herself, in her moral might, to the grand effort which the occasion demands! How would the petty jealousies of the different Protestant sects be swallowed up in the magnitude of the one great enterprise! How would every sect rather cheer the others on, in their united march against the common foe, and make a common rejoicing of the success of any and every corps, as of a victorious regiment in the same great army!

Will American Christians prepare themselves for this enterprise? Will each sect awake to the feeling of its being a corps of the great Christian army, marching under the command of no earthly leader, fighting with no earthly weapons, and against no earthly foe?

Will they wake to the perception of the great truth, that while their great Captain allows each to act separately and independently within certain limits, it is he that commands in chief, and now orders all his soldiers, under whatever earthly banner enrolled, in united phalanx to *go forward*, forward in his single service?

Which corps will first marshal itself for action? Which will be first in the field? Which will press forward with most zeal for the honor of the advance, for the post of danger? Which in the battle will be most in earnest to carry forward the standards of truth and plant them upon the battlements of papal darkness?

Will any shrink back for fear? Will any be deterred from unholy jealousy of its neighbor? Will any indulge in unchristian, ignoble suspicion of its brethren? What cause have any for fear, or jealousy, or suspicion?

This enterprise asks no sacrifice of sectarian principle; it demands no surrender of conscientious predilection of each to its own modes and forms; but it does ask the sacrifice of petty prejudice; it does demand the surrender of those miserable jealousies and envyings which more or less belong to some of every sect, when they learn the greater success of another, as if the victory of one were not the victory of all.

And what are the weapons of this warfare? The Bible, the Tract, the Infant school, the Sunday school, the common school for all classes, the academy for all classes, the college and university for all classes, a free press for the discussion of all questions. These, all these, are weapons of Protestantism, *weapons unknown to Popery!* Yes, all unknown to *genuine* Popery!

Let no one be deceived by the Popish apings of Protestant institutions. The Popish seminary has little in common with the Protestant seminary but the name. It is but the sheep's skin that covers the wolf's back; the teeth and the claws are not even well concealed beneath.

With the weapons we have named, and with our education societies, theological seminaries, and missionary societies, we need no new organization, no Anti-Popery union. But we must use our arms, and not rest satisfied with the possession of them. They must be furbished anew, and we must prepare ourselves for a vigorous warfare. We must be stirring, if we mean indeed to be victorious.

Not a moment is to be lost. The enemy knows well the importance of the present instant. Hear what he says: *"We must make haste, the moments are precious.* IF THE PROTESTANT SECTS ARE BEFOREHAND WITH US, IT WILL BE DIFFICULT TO DESTROY THEIR INFLUENCE."

XI: Duty of the Protestant Community

Ought not this acknowledgment of the enemy to quicken and encourage to instant effort? And again writes a Catholic Missionary:

"Zeal for error is always hot, particularly among the *Methodists*, whom nothing can turn from their track, and who heap absurdity upon absurdity. *I should despair if I should see this sect building a church in my neighborhood.*"

Will not our Methodist brethren take this hint?

†

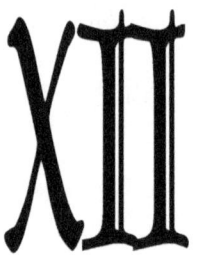# XII | The political duty of American citizens at this crisis

In my last number I deemed it a duty to warn the Christian community against the temptation to which they were exposed, in guarding against the political dangers arising from Popery, of leaving their proper sphere of action, and degrading themselves to a common political interest. This is a snare into which they might easily fall, and into which, if Popery could invite or force them, it might keep a jubilee, for its triumph would be sure. The propensity to resist by unlawful means the encroachment of an enemy, because that enemy uses such means against us, belongs to human nature.

We are very apt to think, in the irritation of being attacked, that we may lawfully hurl back the darts of a foe, whatever may be their character; that we may "fight the devil with fire," instead of the milder,

XII: Political Duty of American Citizens

yet more effective weapon of "the Lord rebuke thee." The same spirit of Christianity which forbids us to return railing for railing, and persecution for persecution, forbids the use of unlawful or even of doubtful means of defense, merely because an enemy uses them to attack us.

If Popery (as is unblushingly the case) organizes itself at our elections, if it interferes politically, and sells itself to this or that political demagogue or party, it should be remembered that this is notoriously the true character of Popery. It is its nature. It cannot act otherwise. Intrigue is its appropriate business.

But all this is foreign to Christianity. Christianity must not enter the political arena with Popery, nor be mailed in Popish armor. The weapons and stratagems of Popery suit not with the simplicity and frankness of Christianity. Like David with the armor of Saul, it would sink beneath the ill-fitting covering, before the Philistine. Yes! Popery will be an overmatch for any Christian who fights behind any other shield than that of Faith, or uses any other sword than the sword of the Spirit of Truth.

But whilst deprecating a *union of religious sects* to act politically against Popery, I must not be misunderstood as recommending no political opposition to Popery by the American community. I have endeavored to rouse Protestants to a renewed and more vigorous use of their religious weapons in their *moral* war with Popery, but I am not unmindful of another duty, the *political* duty, which the double character of Popery makes it necessary to urge upon American citizens with equal force— the imperious duty of defending the distinctive principles of our civil government.

It must be sufficiently manifest to every republican citizen that the civil polity of Popery is in direct opposition to all which he deems sacred in government. He must perceive that Popery cannot, from its very nature, tolerate any of those civil rights which are the peculiar boast of Americans.

Should Popery increase but for a little time longer in this country, with the alarming rapidity with which, as authentic statistics testify, it is advancing at the present time (and it must not be forgotten that despotism in Europe, in its desperate struggles for existence, is lending its powerful aid to the enterprise), we may even in this generation learn, by sad experience, what common sagacity and ordinary research might now teach in time to arrest the evil, that Popery cannot tolerate our form of government in any of its essential principles.

Popery does not acknowledge *the right of the people to govern*; but claims for itself the supreme right to govern all people, and all rulers, by divine right.

It does not tolerate the *Liberty of the Press*; it takes advantage indeed of our liberty of the press to use its own press against our liberty, but it proclaims in the thunders of the Vatican, and with a voice which it pronounces *infallible and unchangeable*, that it is a liberty *"never sufficiently to be execrated and detested."*

It does not tolerate *liberty of conscience* nor *liberty of opinion*. The one is denounced by the Sovereign Pontiff as *"a most pestilential error,"* and the other, *"a pest of all others most to be dreaded in a state."*

It is not responsible to the people in its financial matters. *It taxes at will, and is accountable to none but itself.*

Now these are *political* tenets held by Papists in close union with their religious belief, yet these are not *religious*, but *civil* tenets; they belong to despotic government. Conscience cannot be pleaded against our dealing politically with them. They are separable from religious belief; and if Papists will separate them, and repudiate these noxious principles, and teach and act accordingly, the political duty of exposing and opposing Papists, on the ground of the enmity of their political tenets to our republican government, will cease.

But can they do it? If they can, it behooves them to do it without delay. If they cannot, or will not, let them not complain of *religious* persecution, or of *religious* intolerance, if this republican people, when it shall awake to a sense of the danger that threatens its blood-bought institutions, shall rally to their defense with some show of indignation.

Let them not whine about *religious* oppression, if the democracy turns its searching eye upon this secret treason to the state, and shall in future scrutinize with something of suspicion the professions of those *foreign friends*, who are so ready to rush to a fraternal embrace. Let them not raise the cry of *religious* proscription, if American republicans shall stamp an indelible brand upon the *liveried slaves of a foreign* despot, *the servile adorers of their good "Emperor," the Austrian conspirators,* who now, sheltered behind the shield of our religious liberty, dream of security, while sapping the foundations of our civil government. Let no foreign Holy Alliance presume, or congratulate itself, upon the hitherto unsuspicious and generous toleration of its secret agents in this country.

America may for a time sleep soundly, as innocence is wont to sleep, unsuspicious of hostile attack; but if any foreign power, jealous of the increasing strength of the embryo giant, sends its serpents to lurk within his cradle, let such presumption be assured that the waking energies of the infant are not to be despised; that once having grasped his foes, he will neither be tempted from his hold by admiration of their painted and gilded covering, nor by fear of the fatal embrace of their treacherous folds.

✝

Appendix A

Note A
The War of Opinions

Every account from Europe attests the correctness of the views here taken more than a year since, of the political state of the civilized world.

This war of opinions, or of *categories*, as Lafayette termed it, is in truth commenced, and Americans, if they will but use common observation, cannot but feel that a neglect to notice and provide against the consequences of that settled, systematic hostility to free institutions so strongly manifested by foreign powers, and which is daily assuming a more serious aspect, will inevitably result in mischief to the country, will surely be attended with anarchy, if they wake not to the apprehension of the reality of this danger.

Americans, you indeed sleep upon a mine. This is scarcely a figure of speech; you have excitable materials in the bosom of your society, which, skillfully put in action by artful demagogues, will subvert your present social system; you have a *foreign interest* too, daily, hourly, increasing, ready to take advantage of every excitement, and which will shortly be beyond your control, or will be subdued only by blood. You have agents among you, men in the pay of those very foreign powers, whose every measure of foreign and domestic policy has now for its end and aim *the destruction of liberty everywhere.*

To increase your peril, you have a press that will not apprise you of the dangers that threaten you; we can reach you with our warnings only through the religious journals; the daily press is blind, or asleep, or bribed, or afraid; at any rate, it is silent on this subject, and thus is throwing the weight of its influence on the side of your enemies.

APPENDIX A

Foreign spies have clothed themselves in a religious dress, and so awe-struck are our journalists at its sacred texture, or so unable or unwilling to discern the difference between the man and his mask, that they start away in fear, lest they should be called bigoted or intolerant, or persecuting, if they should venture to lift up the consecrated cloak that hides a foreign foe.

Americans, if you depend on your daily press, you rely on a broken reed; it fails you in your need. It dare not, no, it dare not attack Popery. It dare not drag into the light the *political* enemies of your liberty, because they come in the name of *religion*. All despotic Europe is awake and active in plotting your downfall, and yet they let you sleep, and you choose not to be awaked; "a little more sleep, a little more slumber, a little more folding of the hands to sleep." And now like a man whose house is on fire, dreaming of comfort and security, you will perhaps repel with passion and reproach the friendly hand that would wake you in season to escape with your life.

Do you doubt whether Europe is in hostile array against liberty? Read of the movements and revolutions of foreign cabinets, as one or the other principle temporarily predominates. Read the views of the statesmen of Europe. A distinguished member of the Spanish Cortes, Don Telesforo de Trueba, in a speech delivered before that body a few months since, says:

"The present war is not a war of succession but of principle—*liberty and despotism are at issue*. England, France, Belgium, Spain and Portugal, have ranged themselves under the banner of the former, but it is not necessary for me to name those powers who follow the standard of the latter."

Of Don Carlos and his government, he says:

"Ignorance, hypocrisy, and fanaticism, are his only counsellors, whispering to him new modes of oppressing his people. Everything around is stamped with the marks of baseness and falsehood, while in this infernal region desolation and death reign triumphant. A sanguinary priesthood is sacrificing human victims to the God of peace and love, men who wish to bring back the dark ages, the age of tyranny, and ignorance, and death."

The foreign correspondent of the *Evening Post*, in a letter from Florence, Italy, published in that journal, Dec. 27, 1834, has the following information, directly from Tuscany:

"Hitherto" (in the administration of the government) "a disposition has been shown to let off political offenders as lightly as possible, but lately, however, something of *the same jealousy of republicanism has shown itself, which has been manifested by the other absolute governments of Europe.* A quarterly journal was suppressed a few months since, *on account of something which gave offence to Austria.* This, and several other acts of the Grand Duke, have greatly diminished his personal popularity. The *rulers of Italy appear to have come to an understanding*, that it is time to make an example of some of the disaffected."

Now this Austria is the same busy, meddling government that is operating in this country. We scarcely read the name of Austria in a foreign journal, or in letters from abroad, but in connection with some plan for extinguishing liberty, and yet we harbor her emissaries, promote their secret designs, contribute our money to swell their coffers, build for them their seminaries and convents, entrust our children to their instruction, court their favor, shield them from all attack, yes, even put ourselves under their protection.

All, all this we do, and our native blood flows evenly in our veins. Spirit of '76! Where dost thou sleep?

Note B

Opposite tendencies of Popery and Protestantism

On the very threshold of the examination upon which I have here entered, and while searching among the records of the two sects for the political tendencies of the principles of Popery and Protestantism, I was struck with the marked difference in extent which the two fields of inquiry legitimately offered for examination.

The prime dogma of the Catholics, that all which their church teaches is infallible, unchangeable, that what she has once taught as truth must now and forever be truth, lays open to our examination a wide field. All and each of the precepts, laws, and acts of Popery, from the earliest ages to the present day, may be legitimately quoted to show the political character of that sect. Innovation, repeal, reform, or progress can find no

Appendix A

admittance into the Papal system, without destroying the fundamental principle on which the whole system rests.

"The whole of our faith," says Cardinal Pallavicini, *an infallible authority*, "rests upon one indivisible article, namely the infallible authority of the church. *The moment, therefore, we give up any part whatever, the whole falls*, for what admits not of being divided, must evidently stand entire, or fall entire."

Protestantism, on the contrary, is founded on the Bible; the Bible is the rallying point of all Protestant religious sects. They all believe that God is its author. The religious faith of each is bound to this one volume. But as the Bible prescribes no *form* of faith, or doctrine, or of church government, in which all, in the exercise of the natural and revealed right of private judgment, can agree, each sect adopts that form most in accordance with what it believes to be the spirit of the doctrines which the Bible teaches.

Hence there is diversity of views, according to the diversities of human constitution, according to the varying degrees of intellectual cultivation, or the peculiar wants and condition incident to the infinite variety of circumstances in which human society exists. Upon this freedom to choose according to the dictates of reason and conscience, granted to man by his Maker, denied by Roman Catholics and claimed by Protestants, is built the fabric of *religious liberty*.

Difference of opinion being allowed, *controversy* of course ensues, and converts are to be made not by force of arms, but by force of truth supported by appeals to reason and conscience.

Zealous according to the strength of his belief in the dogmas of his sect, the Protestant calls to his aid all the treasures of science. He believes that the divine Author of truth in the Bible is also the Author of truth in Nature. He knows, that as truth is one, He that created all that forms the vast field of scientific research cannot contradict truth in Scripture by truth in nature; the Protestant is therefore the consistent encourager of all learning, of all investigation. Every discovery in science, he feels, brings to religious truth fresh treasures. Free inquiry, and discussion, all intellectual activity legitimately belong to Protestantism.

It is by thus opening wide the doors of knowledge, and letting in the light of natural science upon what it believes to be the revealed truth of the Bible, that Protestantism has been able gradually to bring out the principle of *religious liberty*, and in its train the invaluable blessing of *civil liberty*.

At the commencement of the Reformation, however, we are not to look for a full development of the free principles of Protestantism. We must expect to find many truths (which, to us who live in the noon of freedom, are as clear as the sun) then obscured or entirely invisible in the popish darkness of the times. The slavish prohibitions, the deep-rooted heathen rites, and the arbitrary dogmas of Popery were then enforced by power, by ignorance, and corruption, so that the struggle of free with despotic principles was attended, through many generations, with constant vicissitude.

No maxim or usage of Popish intolerance, that for a long time clung or still clings to any of the Protestant systems of Europe, can be quoted against *American Protestantism*; consequently I am under no necessity of defending any despotic or intolerant practice, which may be charged or proved upon foreign, or ancient Protestantism; while every act or practice, past or present of Popish enactment is (Papists themselves being judges) available to demonstrate the immutable character of Popery.

NOTE C

The foreign Emissaries of Popery rewarded in their own country

This is a matter deserving of serious attention. Where now is Bishop Cheverus, who passed about fourteen years in Boston? He was a foreigner, with no ties to this country, paid for his services by a foreign government, he had a duty to his foreign masters to perform. What that duty was, may now easily be conjectured.

Boston, as the capital of New England, was considered at the time he arrived, the stronghold of Protestant, of Anti-Popish principles. Popery was there, and throughout New England, held in the greatest abhorrence, for to Popery may be traced, though remotely, yet clearly, the persecutions which drove the Pilgrim fathers to this country. The history of those fathers, for ages previous, is but the history of hard-fought battles, to wrest from Popish usurpation those invaluable rights, civil and religious, which they fled to this wilderness securely to enjoy. Ere popery then could expect to gain foothold among the descendants of the persecuted Puritans, their almost innate abhorrence to popery must be overcome.

What plan could be better devised to accomplish the end, than to send the mild, conciliating, gentle Bishop to demonstrate by his example and his teaching, that Popery was not that monster their fathers had taught them to believe it to be, or at least that now the tyrant had grown mild and tolerant.

If this were the design, no plan could have been more successful. Who that has visited Boston, does not know the epithets with which Bishop Cheverus' name is coupled. The *good Bishop*, the *liberal Bishop*, the *excellent, pious, tolerant, mild* Bishop.

Now all this might have been and perhaps is true of the bishop. The instrument was well chosen, his duty was well accomplished, and he receives the reward of a faithful servant from his foreign masters, in *a translation to the wealthy archbishopric of Bordeaux*.

Again, where is Bishop Dubourg of New Orleans? He has resided in this *heathen* land his stated time, and having accomplished the duty prescribed to him is translated to the Bishopric of Montauban, in France.

And again, where is Bishop Kelly of Richmond, Virginia? He also sojourns with us until his duties to foreign masters are performed, and then is rewarded by promotion at home to the Bishopric of Waterford and Lismore.

And where, soon will be that busy, pompous Jesuit, who has been so often announced as passing and repassing between Rome, Vienna, and the United States, Bishop England? If report speaks truth, he is soon to be rewarded for his services in the cause of his foreign masters with a *Cardinal's hat*.

The following from the *Dublin Freeman's Journal*, preceded by a nauseous mass of fulsome compliment, gives substance to the report:

"After escorting these ladies (some nuns) to Charleston, Dr. England proceeds without delay as Legate from the Pope to Haiti, over the ecclesiastical affairs of which republic he carries with him from the Holy See the most full and unlimited powers; from which we confidently trust, ere long, he will again return to Europe *to receive, as some reward for all his labors and services, a Cardinal's hat;* for, instead of receiving dignity *from*, should such an appointment take place, Dr. England will confer dignity *upon* the sacred purple."

Now in view of these instances of services in this country, rewarded by appointments in Europe, the question naturally occurs: What interest have these servants of a foreign despotism in the free institutions of this country? What sympathies with American liberty can these foreigners have, educated, as they have been in their own country, in the principles of despotic institutions, living but temporarily in this country (whose entire political system is diametrically opposed to their whole education), and looking forward, after their task is performed, to a recall to comfortable benefices and high places of profit and honor at home, to rewards devised by Austria and the Pope, and meted out to their faithful advocates according to the zeal and devotion manifested to their interests?

What would be said of the Episcopalian, or Presbyterian, or Methodist, or Baptist clergy, were they announced as foreigners sent from England, who, after a short sojourn of active service in this country, were known to be recalled and promoted in their own country to be Bishops and dignified officers under the British government?

Note D

Sanguinary spirit still existing in modern Popery

If any suppose that Popery has changed its intolerant character in modern times, we refer them to the following specimen of its spirit. It is Popery of the present day, Popery of 1833.

In the recent journals of Modena, in Italy, are articles signed by the Duke of Canosa, the language of which knows no bounds. He justifies the St. Bartholomew's Massacre. He says:

"When a disease has made such progress, that it cannot be cured by magnesia and calomel, to save life, resort must be had to arsenic. If Charles IX had recoiled from the massacre of the Huguenots, he would certainly have perished, a few weeks after, upon the scaffold, as happened to the indulgent and compassionate Louis XVI, because he took an opposite course. He who in such a case has not the courage of a lion, and does not resolve on rigorous measures, is lost. The pusillanimous alone are ignorant of this truth."

Such shocking sentiments, be it remembered, are published in a country where there is a censorship of the press, and they are therefore the language of the government.

The Duke reasons like a true legitimate. The happiness and lives of the people to any amount, are mere chaff compared with the happiness and life of that sainted bauble called a king. His reasoning amounts to this:

"Better that thousands of the common people should perish by the bloodiest butchery, than that the single life of one human being endowed with *divine right to reign*, should, like Louis XVI perish on the scaffold."

Appendix A

It is not necessary to defend the shedding of royal blood, but there is a trick of kingcraft which ought to be exposed, because its influence is not unfelt in this country. The *divine right* to reign is first assumed, then the human being thus invested with power partakes of *divinity*, he becomes *sacred*, and all the names and paraphernalia of idolatrous worship surround him. He becomes a God; every word he utters, every step he takes, every action, however unimportant in any other human being, is invested in this earthly divinity with a sacred character.

Does the god-king ride out? The whole country must know the important event. Is he married? The whole nation keeps jubilee. Is he dead? The world is clad in mourning. The misfortunes of his offspring are magnified and consecrated by all the arts of the imagination, by all the embellishments of romance.

Is an illustration wanted? Take a recent case.

Look at the history of the Duchess de Berri, an infamous woman, notoriously profligate, of a character that in common life would condemn her to the neglect of the world, and cast her out of all society. But she is a princess, she has a spark of royal divinity that shines upon her brazen front, and the duped multitude bow in adoration before her. Her sufferings, her wanderings, her dress in the minutest particulars, her words, her looks, are the subject of sympathetic appeals to the compassion of the world; ladies shed tears over the distresses of the unfortunate princess.

Alas! Alas! That royal blood should suffer! And are we not influenced by this mawkish, morbid sympathy for suffering despots? Where are our sympathies, when the interested statements of a government-controlled foreign press, inform us of the struggles of the people against age-consecrated oppression? Are they with *the people?*

Do we ever suspect the truth of the glowing details of the doings of the *scandalous mob*, the high-wrought accounts of outrage and rebellion of a *wicked rabble* against *lawful authority*, which circulate through our land, the production abroad of pensioned writers; of a licensed press, and those too without remark or explanation from our press?

What should be the feelings of a true American? Where should be his sympathies, who has been nurtured in the air of liberty, who has learned from his father's lips the black catalogue of despotic wrongs, which his ancestors suffered, and which were defended by all the tricks and glosses, and arts of oppression? If any human being should feel quick sympathy with the struggles of the *people*, should examine with the greatest care the charges preferred against them, and exercise a willing charity for their apparent or real excesses, and quick mistrust of all the doings, representations and fair speeches of *despotism*, it is an American.

Note E

Popery is organized throughout the World

This organization is asserted in the late proclamation of the Pope to the Portuguese. In the catalogue of his complaints he says:

"Nevertheless, that which principally afflicts us is, that those acts and measures have evidently for their aim to break every bond of union, with that venerable chair of the blessed Peter" (his own throne) "which Jesus Christ has made the center of unity; and thus the society of communion being once broken, to wound the church by the most pernicious schism. In fact, how can there be unity in the body, when the members are not united to the head, and do not obey it?"

Note F

Emigration and our Naturalization Law

The subject of *emigration* is one of those which demands the immediate attention of the nation, it is a question which concerns all parties; and if the writer is not mistaken in his reading of the signs of the times, the country is waking to a sense of the alarming evil produced by our *naturalization* laws.

Let us war among ourselves in party warfare, with every lawful weapon that we can convert to our purpose. It is our birthright to have our own opinion, and earnestly to contend for it, but let us court no *foreign* friends.

Every American should feel his national blood mount at the very thought of foreign interference. While we welcome the intelligent and persecuted of all nations and give them an asylum and a share in our privileges, let us beware lest we admit to dangerous fellowship those who cannot and will not use our hospitality aright.

That such may come, and do come, there is no reason to doubt. Consider the following testimony of an emigrant, given before a justice in Albany. He says that "in June last, the *parish officers* paid the passages of himself and about *forty others of the same parish*, from Chatham to the city of Boston, in America, on board the ship *Royalist*, Capt. Parker, and that they landed in Boston in the month of July last, that the parish officers gave him thirty shillings sterling, in money, in addition to paying his passage—that he is now entirely destitute of the means of living, and is unable to labor, and prays for relief."

Now here are *forty paupers* cast upon our shores from one parish in England, and in *five years* they become citizens, *entitled to vote!* Is there an American of any party, who can believe that there is no danger in admitting to equal privileges with himself such a class of foreigners? A remedy to this crying evil admits of not a moment's delay. At this moment the ocean swarms with ships crowded with this wretched population, bearing them from misery abroad to misery here.

The expense incurred in this city (New York) for the support of foreign paupers, it is well known is enormous. In Philadelphia more than *three-fourths* of the inmates of their Almshouse are *foreigners*. Whole families have been known to come from on board ship, and go directly to the Almshouse.

In the Boston Dispensary there were the last year (1831), from two districts only, *477 patients; of these 441 were foreigners!* Leaving but 36 of our own population to be provided for. In the Boston Almshouse, the following returns show the increase of foreign paupers in *five years:*

The year ending Sept. 30, 1829	— Americans 395
	— Foreigners 284
The year ending Sept. 30, 1834	— Americans 340
	— Foreigners 613

Thus we see that native pauperism has decreased in five years, and foreign pauperism more than doubled.

In Cambridge (Mass.), more than *four-fifths* of the paupers are foreigners.

The first and immediate step that should be taken, is to press upon Congress and upon the nation, instant attention to the NATURALIZATION LAWS. We mast first stop this leak in the ship, through which the muddy waters from without threaten to sink us. If we mean to keep our country, this lifeboat of the world, from foundering with all the crew, we must take on board no more from the European wreck until we have safely landed and sheltered its present freight.

But would you have us forfeit the character of the country as the asylum of the world? No, but it is a mistaken philanthropy indeed that would attempt to save one at the expense of the lives of thousands; that would receive into our families those dying of the plague. Our naturalization laws were never intended to convert this land into the almshouse of Europe, to cover the alarming importation of everything in the shape of man that European tyranny thinks fit to send adrift from its shores, nor so to operate as to compel us to surrender back all the blessings of that freedom for which our fathers paid so dear a price into the keeping of its foreign enemies.

No, we must have the law so amended that NO FOREIGNER WHO MAY COME INTO THE COUNTRY, AFTER THE PASSAGE OF THE NEW LAW, SHALL EVER BE ALLOWED TO EXERCISE THE ELECTIVE FRANCHISE. This alone meets the evil in its fullest extent.

Who can complain of injustice in the enactment of such a law? Not the *native American*, he is not touched by it. Certainly not the *foreigner now in the country*, whether naturalized or not. It cannot operate against him. It would take away *no right* from a *single individual* in any country. This law would withhold a *favor*, not a right from foreigners, and from those foreigners only who may hereafter come into the country. If foreigners abroad choose to take offense at the law, we are not under obligations to consult their wishes, they need not come here. This favor, it should be understood, has repeatedly been abused, and it is necessary for the safety of our institutions in future to withhold it.

The pressing dangers to the country from Popery, which I think I have shown not to be fictitious; other visible indications of foreign influence in the political horizon; the bold organization of foreigners as foreigners in our elections—these, all demand the instant attention of Americans, if they mean not to be robbed, by foreign intrigue, of their liberty, and their very name.

NOTE G

One College at the West under Austrian influence

The following fact illustrates the dangerous, successful intriguing spirit of the Jesuits, and the culpable negligence of one of our state legislatures (that of Kentucky) who has thus suffered itself to be the dupe of Popish artifice. St. Joseph's College, at Bardstown, Kentucky, was incorporated by the State Legislature in 1824.

The Bishop of Bardstown is Moderator, and five Priests are Trustees. And there is this provision in the charter:

> "The said trustees shall hold their station in said college one year only, at which time the said moderator shall have the power of electing others, or the same, if he should think proper, and increase the number to twelve, and this power may be exercised by him every year thereafter, or his successor or successors to the Bishopric; and in case of the removal, resignation or death of either of the said trustees, his place may be supplied by an appointment that may be made by the said Bishop, or his successor or successors, who may also become moderators in the institution, and act and do as the said B.J. Flaget is empowered by this act to do."

The Bishop of Bardstown, in a letter to a friend in Europe, dated February, 1825, says:

"Our legislature has just incorporated the college. The Bishops of Bardstown are continued perpetually its moderators or rectors. *I might have dictated conditions*, which I could not have made more advantageous or honorable; and what is still more flattering is, that these privileges were granted almost without any discussion, and with unanimity in both houses."

Now the Pope it is well known appoints all Bishops. Here then is one college in the country already placed *in perpetuo* under the exclusive control of the Pope, and consequently for an indefinite period under that of Austria!

Note H

Glory-Giving Titles

One of the plainest doctrines of American Republicanism, which is essentially democratic, is, that mere glory-giving titles, or titles of servility, are entirely opposed to its whole spirit. They are considered as one of those artificial means of kingcraft by which it fosters that aristocratic, unholy pride in the human heart, which loves to domineer over its fellow man, which loves artificial distinction of ranks, a privileged class, and of course which helps to sustain that whole system of regal and papal usurpation which has so long cursed mankind.

If such titles are to some extent still acknowledged in this country, they have either been thoughtlessly but unwisely used as mere epithets of courtesy, or they are the remains of old deep-rooted foreign habits, which, in spite of the uncongenial soil to which they have been transplanted, still maintain a sort of withered existence.

It now, however, becomes a serious inquiry, whether this practice, hitherto seemingly unimportant, may not be attended with danger to the institutions of the country. For Popery, it appears, is already taking advantage of this, as of all other weaknesses in our habits and customs, to introduce its anti-democratic system, and this too while it manifests in words great zeal in defense of democratic liberty. Let the democracy look well to this.

Is it asked, to what extent should titles or names of distinction be abolished throughout the land, the answer is plain.

Every title that merely designates an office, is perfectly in accordance with our institutions, such as President, Secretary, Senator, General, Commodore, &c. So are letters after a name which designate the office or membership in a society, but titles of reverence, titles which imply moral qualities, such as Your Excellency, Your Honor, The Reverend, Rt. Reverend, Honorable, &c.; and letters which imply moral or intellectual superiority, I think it must be conceded are now not only useless but dangerous.

There needs no law to abolish these gewgaw appendages to a name; they must be left to the good sense of the individual who uses them, to discontinue them; and fortunately they generally belong to intellectual men, who have minds capable of discerning the remote evils to which the practice leads, and patriotism enough to make a greater sacrifice than this occasion calls for to avert dangers which threaten their country.

Will it be said that this is a little matter? Nothing is of little consequence that may endanger, however remotely, the civil liberty of the country. Nay more, no practice is unworthy of reform, which, continued, may aid by its example in the surrender of Religious liberty into the hands of Popery.

Appendix A

Note I
Compulsory Baptism

Perhaps Father Baraga was thinking of the facilities afforded in Spain in the time of Ximenes for administering baptism, when "Fifty thousand (50,000) Moors, under terror of death and torture, received the grace of baptism, and more than an equal number of the refractory were condemned, of whom 2,536 were burnt alive." May our government long be *"too free"* for the enacting of such barbarity.

Notes J & K
Priests control the Mob

If no farther proof were wanting of the fact of the supreme influence of the Catholic priests over the mob, it is opportunely furnished in the testimony on the trial of the rioters at Charlestown, Mass.

Mr. Edward Cutter testified that the Lady Superior, in an interview previous to the burning of the convent, thus threatened him; she said, "the Bishop had 20,000 of the vilest (or boldest) Irishmen under his control, who would tear down the houses of Mr. Cutter and others; and that the selectmen of Charlestown might read the riot act till they were hoarse, and it would be of no use."

But if any doubt is thrown over Mr. Cutter's testimony because he is a Protestant, hear what the Lady Superior herself testifies.

"I told him," she says, that "the Right Reverend Bishop's influence over ten thousand *brave* Irishmen might lead to the destruction of his property, and that of others."

Here we have the startling fact, acknowledged in a court of justice by the Superior of the convent, that the Bishop has such influence over a mob of foreigners, that he can use them for vengeance or restrain them at pleasure. The question that occurs is, how much stronger is it necessary for this foreign corps to become, before it may prudently act offensively against our noxious Protestant institutions?

The fact is established by Catholic testimony, that the Popish population is not an *unorganized* mob, but is moved by priestly leaders, Jesuit foreigners in the pay of Austria. They are ready to keep quiet or to strike as circumstances may render expedient. But exclusive of other proof, another most important fact is rendered certain by this singular confession of the Lady Superior, and that is *Roman Catholic interference in our elections.*

Jesuits are not in the habit of slighting their advantages, and the Bishop who can control ten or twenty thousand, or five hundred thousand men, as the case may be, for the purpose of destruction and riot, can certainly *control the votes* of these obedient instruments! Will not American freemen wake to the apprehension of a truth like this?

Note L
Political interference of Popery

The kind of interference in the political affairs, of other countries by the *Sovereign of Rome*, may be learned from the following extracts from the Pope's Proclamation against Don Pedro in which he thus speaks of Portugal.

He laments the defection of "that kingdom, cited, until now, as a model of devotion and of fidelity to the Catholic faith, to the Holy See, and to the Roman pontiffs, our predecessors; a kingdom which, as is meet, has already felt it an honor to obey its Sovereigns, distinguished by the title of *Most faithful Kings*.

"We confess that we could not at first believe what report and public rumor related upon enterprises so audacious, but the unexpected return to Italy of him who represented us in the said kingdom as Apostolic Nuncio, and the most positive testimony of many persons, soon convinced us that what had been previously announced to us was but too true.

"It is then as certain as it is greatly to be deplored, that the above-mentioned Government has unjustly driven away him who *represented our person* and the Holy See, commanding him to quit the kingdom without delay. But after so gross an insult offered to the Holy See, and to us, the audacity of these perverse men bas been carried still further against the Catholic Church, against ecclesiastical property, against the inviolable rights of the Holy See.

"Considering that all these measures have been exercised, almost at the accession of a new Power, and in consequence of a conspiracy prepared beforehand, our mind is filled with horror, and we cannot refrain from tears. All the public prisons have been opened, and, after having let those who were detained there go forth, they have thrown into them, in their place, some of those of whom it is written, *Touch not*

Appendix A

my Anointed. Laymen have rashly arrogated to themselves a power over sacred things; they have proclaimed a general reform of the secular clergy, and of religious orders of both sexes."

After enumerating various acts of rigor of the new government against those priests, monks and other ecclesiastics, who had taken an active part in the civil war, the Pope continues:

"For this reason, venerable brethren, we expressly proclaim that *we absolutely reprobate all the decrees issued by the aforesaid government of Lisbon*, to the great detriment of the Church, of its holy ministers, of the ecclesiastical law, and Holy See prerogatives; *we, therefore, declare them to be null and of no effect*, and express our most serious complaints against the audacious measures we have referred to; we declare that in *exercising the duties of our office*, and with God's help, *we will oppose ourselves as a wall for the House of Israel, and show ourselves in the combat at the day of the Lord, as the interests of religion and the gravity of circumstances may require*."

He hopes this low rumbling of the thunders of the Vatican will prevent his "having recourse to those spiritual arms with which God has invested his apostolic ministry," namely anathemas, curses of excommunication, &c. And these are not the records of doings of the dark ages, but are fresh from the papal throne, the acts of 1833.

Note M

If any suppose that Popery meddles not with *civil matters in this country*, let them peruse the following extract of a letter from one of their missionaries:

> Mr. Baraga to the Central Direction of the Leopold Foundation,
> Dated L'Arbre Croche, October 10th, 1832. On the 5th of August, after partaking the sacrament of confirmation, the bishop called all the chiefs and head men of the mission, and made known to them some *civil laws*, which he had made for the Ottowas. The Indians received these laws with much pleasure, and promised solemnly to obey them. *The missionary and four chiefs are the administrators of these laws.*
> Frederick Baraga, Missionary.

Here is a specimen of the disposition of Popery to meddle in civil matters in this country where it has the power: the Bishop is the propounder, and the missionary one of the administrators of the civil laws.

Note N

The poor, the illiterate, and the working classes the most deeply interested in quelling riot and disorder

I have elsewhere hinted at the danger to the stability of our institutions of the *mob spirit* which has been manifested in different parts of the country. But I fear that the *process of disorganization*, the gradual change which frequent riot necessarily works in the nature of government has not been duly considered by those whom it most deeply, most vitally concerns; I mean the *hardworking, uneducated poor*. Let me endeavor to trace this process.

What is the proper effect of our democratic republican institutions upon the various classes into which human society must ever be divided? How do they affect the condition of the *rich* and the *poor*, the *educated* and the *illiterate*?

Equality, the only practicable equality, is their result; not that spurious, visionary equality which would make a forced community of property, but that equality which puts no *artificial* obstacles in the way of any man's becoming the richest or most learned in the state; which allows every man without other impediment than the common obstacles of human nature and the equal rights of his neighbor impose, to strive after wealth and knowledge and happiness.

True Christian republicanism, by its benevolent and ennobling principles, impels the wealthy and the educated to use their talents for the benefit of the whole community; it prompts to acts of public spirit, to self-sacrifice, and to unwearied effort to lessen the natural obstacles in the way of the poor and uneducated to competence and intellectual character, by affording them both employment and education.

The kindness and benevolence thus shown to the poor beget in this class of our citizens, industry and mental effort. They feel that they are not like the proscribed of other countries, they see that the way is equally open to all to rise to the same rank of independence in mind and condition, and they consequently are without the exciting causes of envy and ill-will and bitterness of feeling towards the wealthy and educated, which exist and produce these fruits in other and arbitrary governments.

Society in its two extremes is thus knit together by a mutual confidence, and a mutual interest, for causes beyond human control are ever varying the condition of men. He that is rich today may be poor tomorrow; and thus there is a constant interchange, a mingling of ranks, which like a healthful circulation in the natural body, begets soundness and vigor through the political body. The vicious, and voluntarily ignorant being the only portions of society naturally and justly excluded from the benefits of this system.

Let us now look at the condition of these same classes under an arbitrary government. In Austria, for example, the *poor* and *illiterate* are considered as the natural slaves of the *wealthy* and *learned*. These classes are perpetually separated by the artificial barrier of *hereditary right*; the line of separation is distinctly drawn, and in all that relates to social intercourse there is an impassable gulf.

There may be condescension on the one part, but no elevation on the other. High birth, learning, wealth, and polished manners are on the one side, strengthening the hands of the arbitrary power that sustains them; on the other, low birth, ignorance, poverty, and boorishness, kept down by their intrinsic weakness, generation after generation in irretrievable subjection; the upper classes knowing that their own security is based upon the perpetuity of ignorance and superstition in the lower classes.

Now to make the change from republicanism to absolutism, what means would an arbitrary power like Austria be most likely to devise? Would she not attain her object entirely by the creation on the one hand, in the wealth and talent of this country, a necessity for employing physical force to hold in subjection the poor and illiterate? And the production, on the other hand, of a class ignorant and unprincipled, and turbulent enough to need the very restraints the other class might be compelled to employ? Are there any indications of such a change in this country?

We have a daily increasing host of emigrants, a portion of the very class used to foreign servitude abroad. How could Austrian emissaries better serve their imperial master's interests, than by keeping these unenlightened men in the same mental darkness in which they existed in the countries from which they came, surrounding them here with a police of priests, and shutting out from them the light which might break in upon them in this land of light, nourishing them for riot and turbulence, at political meetings, and for bullying at the polls those of opposite political opinions?

And what would be the effect of such a mode of proceedings upon that class, who have acquired by lives of honest industry and studious application, wealth, and knowledge, and political experience?

Is not such a course calculated to drive them away from any participation in the politics of the country, and is not such seditious conduct intended to produce this very result?

Will not men who have any self-respect, who have any sense of character, turn away and ask with feelings of indignation, where is that intelligent, sober, orderly body of *native* mechanics and artisans, who once composed the wholesome, substantial democracy of the country, and on whose independence and rough good sense the country could always rely—that well-tried body of their own fellow-citizens, accustomed to hear and read patiently, and decide discreetly?

And when they see them associated with a rude set of priest-governed foreigners, strangers to the order and habits of our institutions, requiting us for their hospitable reception by conduct subversive of the very institutions which make them freemen; when they see them become the dupes of the machinations of a foreign despotic power, refusing to be undeceived, and madly rushing to their own destruction, will they not from motives of self-preservation be willing to adopt any system of measures, however arbitrary, which will secure society from violence and anarchy?

When disgust at priest-guided mobs shall have alienated the minds of one class of the citizens from the other, we have then *one of the parties* nearly formed, which is necessary for the designs of despotism in accomplishing the subversion of the republic. And *the other party* is still easier formed.

The alienation of feeling in the wealthier class, and their remarks of disgust, may be easily tortured into contempt for the classes below them, and then the natural envy of the poor towards the rich, will always furnish occasions to excite to violence. When hostility between these two parties has reached a proper height, the signal from the arch jugglers in Europe to their assistants here, can easily kindle the flames of civil strife.

And then comes the dexterous change of systems. Frequent outrage must be quelled by military force, for the public peace must at all events be preserved, and the civil arm will have become too weak, and thus commences an *armed police*, itself but the precursor of a standing army.

And which party will be the sufferer? All experience answers that *wealth* and *talent* are more than a match for mere brute force, for the plain reason that they can both *purchase* and *direct* it. The rich can pay for their protection, and soldiers belong to those who pay them. The man of talent is wanted to direct, and he also is retained by the rich. What then becomes of the illiterate and laboring poor? Reduced after ineffectual, ill-concerted resistance to the same state of perfect subjection that obtains in the *"happy Austrian empire."* It is the *poor*, then, the *poor* and *ignorant*, not the rich and learned, that have everything of hope and liberty to lose from the machinations of Austria.

In a moral and intelligent Democracy, the rich and poor are friends and equals, in a Popish despotism the poor are in abject servitude to the rich. Let the working men, the laboring classes, well consider that their liberty is in danger, and can be preserved only by their encouragement of education and good order.

Note O

Dangers from a riotous spirit, and the kind of treatment due from Protestant Americans to Catholic Emigrants

All the topics which grow out of this momentous subject of Popery as their prolific parent, are of absorbing national interest, but no one forces itself upon our consideration more imperiously at this moment than that which heads this note.

For, unless I am greatly deceived, the waking up of this great nation's indignation, the shaking off of the lethargy which has so long held in unaccountable stupor the senses of the people, which has shut their eyes and stopped their ears to the proofs of foreign conspiracy which everywhere surrounded them, the mighty gathering of all real patriots to the defense of their liberties, which the sounds of preparation from all quarters of the land but too strongly indicate, may be attended with effects disastrous to the cause of true liberty, may produce through excess or ill-regulated zeal, the evil which it is desirous to remedy.

For excess even in favor of right principles, doubles the amount of the evil which it attempts to cure. Excess of all kinds, whether in thought, word, or action (Oh! that this could be impressed on every American heart) is just so much gain to the side of Popery.

I know not how prevalent is error on this point, but I am persuaded that it exists to an extent to make an American tremble for the permanency of our democratic institutions.

Is there not a culpable acquiescence in the doings of a mob, if their violence is directed against some apparent or real irritating popular evil? Is not the language of such acquiescence most dangerous?

It amounts to this: "Although we are averse to mob law, yet on the whole there are cases where the sin is venial, and the character of the nuisance it would abate justifies its violence."

Now once concede in a democratic community, a community which makes its own laws according to modes prescribed by itself, that an irresponsible minority may set at defiance these laws, and then let me ask, where is government? It is prostrated. It has become anarchy, and on the ruins of social order will arise another form of government more or less *arbitrary*, according to the more or less profound causes which effected the destruction of the first.

Of all forms of government, a truly democratic government, while it is least obnoxious to the disturbing influences of mobs, can at the same time least of all bear the shocks of their turbulence.

No events, therefore, that have occurred in the eventful history of the country, have so justly caused alarm for the stability of the government, as the spirit of mob violence which has lately manifested itself so frequently in our large cities. We should do well to remember that we have secret and artful enemies busily at work, who can and will take advantage of this unnatural state of the public feeling, and who will not fail secretly to administer fuel, in modes in which they are perfectly familiar, to a diseased excitement so favorable to their views.

We have in the country a powerful religious-politico sect, whose final success depends on the subversion of these democratic institutions, and who have therefore a vital interest in promoting mob-violence.

The saying of the German ambassador concerning the Papists (quoted in the prefatory remarks) is full of meaning, and should be constantly borne in mind; it lets us into the secret of much of their maneuvering in this country; *"they will be hammer or nails, they will persecute or be persecuted."*

Where they are in power, they always persecute; when not in power and consequently unable to persecute, they will be sure to conduct, either in so outrageous or mysterious, or deceptive a manner, *as to rouse public indignation.* They will contrive ingenious modes of irritation that shall draw upon them popular vengeance, and then all meekness and innocence, and resignation, raise the imploring cry of persecution.

And how do they gain by these opposite modes? If they are strong enough to persecute, they will destroy their opponents, *in obedience to the openly avowed principles of their sect,* by exile, by dungeons, and by death.

If they themselves are persecuted in a Protestant community (Protestant principles being in known direct opposition to persecution), it is always by an *irreligious mob, acting in defiance of Protestant principle,* and unsustained by public opinion, and the reaction of Protestant sympathy for the sufferers on any such occasion, more than makes amends by its gifts for the injury sustained. Thus the very virtues of Protestants growing out of principles directly antagonist to Popish principles, are made to work against Protestantism, and in favor of Popery.

Do not Jesuits know the well-known truth, that a sect is helped by a little persecution? Do they not now act upon a knowledge of it?

And should not Americans replenish their memory with it also, that they may most rigidly abstain from disorder, and discountenance every disposition to riot or violence? Let them remember that the laws that govern them are their own laws, and they must not allow them to be broken. Let them suspect a Popish plot to rob them of their liberties in every disorderly assemblage, and by good order, by firmness of resistance to every temptation to riot, defeat the designs of these worst enemies of Democracy.

In close connection with this topic, is that of *the kind of treatment which Protestant Americans should show to Catholic emigrants?* On this subject a volume could be written. I have space but for a few remarks.

The condition of the Catholic emigrants that are daily pouring into the country from Germany and Ireland should awaken the strongest sympathies of Americans; and in whatever aspect viewed, should enlist all their feelings of benevolence.

Reflect a moment who and what they are. We have read, and our own countrymen who have travelled and seen them in their native land, bear testimony to the effects upon the people of the grinding oppressions of Papal government; to the mental degradation, to the poverty, to the wretchedness of the vassals of despotism. And as if to prove to us what we might doubt on the authority of others, so somber is their picture of human misery, the very subjects of foreign oppression are brought and placed before our eyes.

See yonder ship slowly furling her sails. She approaches the city. She casts her anchor. Who are those that crowd her decks?

With eager eyes they gaze in one direction. They see at length the far-famed land of liberty. Yes, its name has been wafted even to their ears, and with the longings of captives for freedom they have broken away from slavery and sought the asylum of the oppressed. They land upon our shores.

Look, Americans, see before you the fruits of *papal education!*—of papal care of the bodies and minds of its children. Filthy and ragged in body, ignorant in mind, and but too often most debased in morals, they fill your streets with squalid beggary, and your highways with crime; they are such a loathsome picture of degradation, moral and physical, that you turn away in disgust from the sight.

But why should this be? They are human beings, although oppression has blotted out their reason and conscience and thought. They are the progeny of Popery; they are the victims of its iron despotism. It is Popery that has reared them up in its own caverns of superstition.

They exhibit before you the blighting effects of this scourge of the earth. It is Popery that has filled their minds with puerile fables, closed their mental eyes in the darkness of ignorance, fleeced them of their property by systematic robbery, kept them from the knowledge of their natural rights as men to liberty of conscience, and of opinion, extorted an abject obedience to their fellow-men, to blasphemous usurpers of the prerogatives of Deity.

Their ignorance is their lasting, fatal curse, their reason and conscience stifled at their birth, they are cast upon our care mere human machines, for the fell usurpers of God's power have torn out of them their very minds. To think for themselves, that inalienable right of a rational being, is rebellion against their priest; they read not, they understand not our charter of liberty.

They love liberty, indeed, but what shape has liberty to men without minds? What perception of light has a sightless eye? Their liberty is licentiousness; their freedom, strife and debauchery.

And now with what emotions should Protestants look on these suffering, deluded men? In what channel should their sympathies flow? They have already been beaten to the dust by tyranny. Is it for freemen to follow up the cruel blow of foreign tyrants? They have been brutalized by neglect; shall they now be hunted by proscription? Shall no Christian effort be made to light up again in their darkened bosoms the extinguished spark of humanity?

They are followed into our habitations. Yes, Americans, they are pursued into your own asylum of liberty by their foreign oppressors, who, like hungry wolves, have ventured with unhallowed feet into the very sanctuary of freedom to grasp again their scarcely escaped prey.

And have Americans no compassion? Have they no courage? Will they not protect the oppressed? Will they not interpose between them and their priestly oppressors, and say to the latter:

"Stand off; this is a land of freedom; these men are now American citizens; they have a right to American education; to republican education; to Bible education. They have a right to the knowledge that they owe no allegiance to priests, that here there are no forbidden books, that knowledge here is not meted out in scanty drops to serve the purposes of power-grasping despots, but is spread out before them wide and deep as the ocean; that American laws protect them from *ecclesiastical* as well as civil *proscription*, from *ecclesiastical* as well as civil *extortion*; that they owe no obligation to pay an arbitrary tax of bishop or priest, that they have a right to know the *amount, and the manner of disbursement, of every cent they are called on to contribute in church* as well as state?"

Will not Americans teach them these truths, and aid them to break the chains with which foreign tyrants have bound them? Or will they compel them, by proscription and persecution, or unfeeling neglect, to clan together around their priests, because deserted by those who should, and who alone can, undeceive and enlighten them?

In the one case there is hope of incorporating them into the American republican family as useful fellow citizens. In the other, there is the certainty of perpetuating a distinct foreign and hostile interest in the country, to distract its councils, to sully the peaceful character of its institutions, and finally to aid in the complete destruction of this stronghold, this last hope of Freedom.

> ——but once put out thy (light,)
> Thou cunning'st pattern of excelling nature,
> I know not where is the Promethean heat
> That can thy light relume.

Note P

Both political Parties intrigue for Catholic votes

Let neither political party throw upon its antagonist the exclusive odium of courting this foreign, priest-disciplined band. There are some of both parties who must hide their heads with shame, when real Americans, the patriots of the country, disregarding party name, shall turn their indignant eyes upon this lurking enemy of liberty, and shall apprehend the reality of this foreign conspiracy.

Is either political party disposed to upbraid the other with tampering with Popery, or to congratulate itself that it has kept its own garments unspotted front the crime of this indirect treason? If either thus flatters itself, *let it be dumb;* let guilt stop the utterance of both. Both are deplorably, *notoriously* guilty. This is a truth that cannot and will not be denied.

Both have bargained with these organized vassals of a foreign power. Both in their eager recklessness to triumph over each other, have aided foreign despotism to prostrate at its feet the liberties of their country, the liberties of the world.

All parties, religious and political, are suffering, and have yet much more to suffer from the evils already produced by this their blind folly, by their culpable servility to priest-governed foreigners, their cowardly backwardness in not daring to drag into the light this covert treason, because, forsooth, it comes in a sacred garb, their wretchedly loose notions of tolerance, and charity and liberality, their shameful disregard of the consequences of their bargainings.

And is it indeed come to this? A nation of Protestant freemen, nurtured in Protestant principles, the only true principles of liberty, principles wrested from tyranny by the persevering valor of their fathers, the result of the intellectual, aye, and physical combats of centuries—the fruits of obstinately contested struggles with despotism, and superstition, and bigotry—struggles of ages against the united intrigues of kingcraft and priest-craft.

Americans, thus emancipated, having enjoyed the peaceful fruits of these blood-earned truths for two centuries, at length grow careless of their treasure. They sport with their liberty as if it were nothing worth; they grow weary of guarding their happiness, they sleep on their posts, they settle down into quiet security. They have ships, and forts, and arms, and brave hearts to defend their shores, and so there is no danger—all is peace, for the battle has long since been won, they can now safely doff their armor, there is no further need of the watchings of the camp.

Our enemies, they say, have in truth become our friends: Kings are now Republican, and the Pope, yes the Pope (his bulls and proclamations to the contrary notwithstanding), we hope and believe has turned a Protestant Republican, at least in this country. Let us be generous, say these descendants of ever jealous sires, let us invite our former foes to partake of our hospitality. How noble the sentiment! How will the world applaud! Let us show an example of liberality unparalleled.

The invitation is accepted, and they flock in countless thousands to our shores; a motley band, the oppressor and the oppressed together, and their relations to each other too unchanged.

They have needed no Trojan Horse to hide them from our too credulous eyes; we lead them openly into the midst of us. They parade our streets with foreign banners, already they flaunt them in our faces in derision.

They even threaten us with their vengeance, and we cower beneath their frown. Yes, we plead with them to spare us, we thank them for restraining their rod, we humbly confess the sins of our ancestors, we tell them our fathers were *bigoted* and *fanatical*, they were *too prejudiced* against these our regal and papal friends.

We, their children, grown more liberal, will show our freedom from narrow prejudices; we will make amends for past offences. Our papal friends shall be received with open arms.

We will even urge them to be the umpires in our family quarrels; we will beseech them to educate our children in their foreign principles of passive obedience. We will build for them their fortresses on our own soil, to attack our own strong holds, and then we will trust to their mercy.

We shall then have delivered up to them all the keys of our house, and what will remain for us but to bow our necks beneath the foot of the Pope, and asking absolution for our own sins, and our father's sins of long rebellion against his rightful sovereignty, humbly beg a legal charter for our country, and a consecrated king for our throne?

Note Q

Popish experiment on the Military of the Country

The experiments of Popery in various parts of the country on the ignorance or credulity, or apathy of the people, are every day, I might say every hour, more manifest, and they are prosecuted with a boldness, with an audacious defiance of American habits, and the feelings of American Republicanism, truly astonishing.

Yet upon reflection, is it so astonishing that a tyranny of such inexhaustible resources of cunning and artifice, backed by the treasures, and the open encouragement of the arbitrary governments of Europe, should be more than ordinarily bold? For if success attends the advance of these arch intriguers against our Protestant habits and institutions, high honors and pecuniary rewards await them at home—if detection at any time overtakes them from the sudden waking of their victim, and his restive efforts to break off the bands that they would spider-like softly bind upon him—they have a retreat from punishment in their own country.

A new experiment, another step forward in the march against our freedom (and to all appearances, at present, a successful one), has been tried at the West, at St. Louis, in the consecration of the Popish cathedral. The account is from a Popish Journal, called the *Catholic Telegraph*. They shall have the benefit of their own recital:

> The Cathedral of St. Louis is 134 feet long by 84 wide. There are 8 rows of pews, 25 in each row, calculated to contain at least 8,000 persons. There are two magnificent colonnades at opposite sides in the body of the church, consisting of five massive pillars, of brick, elegantly marbled, and each four feet in diameter.
>
> The altar is of stone. It is only temporary, and will soon be superseded by a superb marble altar, which is hourly expected from Italy.
>
> The church it is said has already cost $42,000. It is presumed that about $18,000 more will be required to finish it, according to the original and magnificent design of its founders; so that the entire cost of the building and its furniture cannot be less than $60,000.

Appendix A

The consecration took place on the Sabbath, October 26, 1834.

At an early hour, 7 A.M. on the day of consecration, four Bishops, twenty-eight Priests—twelve of whom were from TWELVE different nations—and a considerable number of young aspirants to the holy ministry, making the entire ecclesiastical corps amount to fifty or sixty, were habited in their appropriate dresses.

As *soon as the procession was organized*, the pealing of three large and clear-sounding bells, *the thunder of two pieces of artillery* raised all hearts, as well as our own to the Great Almighty Being.

When the HOLY RELICS were moved towards their new habitation, where they shall enjoy an anticipated resurrection—the presence of their God in His holy tabernacle, *the guns fired a second salute*. We felt as if the soul of ST. LOUIS, Christian, Lawgiver and HERO, was in the sound, and that he again led on *his victorious armies* in the service of the God of Hosts, for the defense of his religion, his sepulcher, and his people.

When the solemn moment of the consecration approached, and the *Son of the living God* was going to descend for the *first time*, into the new residence of his glory on earth, the *drums* beat the *reveille, three of the star-spangled banners were lowered over* the balustrade of the sanctuary, the *artillery* gave a *deafening discharge*.

The dedication sermon was preached by the Bishop of Cincinnati. *During the Divine Sacrifice, two of the military* stood with *drawn swords,* one at each side of the *altar;* they belonged to a *guard of honor* formed *expressly* for the occasion. Besides whom, there were detachments from the four militia companies of the city, the *Marions*, the *Grays*, the *Riflemen*, and the *Cannoneers from Jefferson Barracks, stationed at convenient distances around the church.*

Well and eloquently did the Rev. Mr. Abell, pastor of Louisville, observe in the evening discourse, alluding to his own and the impressions of the clergy and laity, who were witnesses to the scene:

> "Fellow Christians and Fellow Citizens! I have seen the flag of my country proudly floating at the masthead of our richly freighted merchantmen; I have seen it fluttering in the breeze at the head of our armies, but never, *never* did my heart *exult*, as when I this day behold it, for the first time, bow before its God!
>
> "Breathing from infancy the air which our artillery had purified from the infectious spirit of bigotry and persecution, it would be the pride of my soul, to take the brave men by the hand, by whom these cannons were served. But for these cannons, there would be no home for the free, no asylum for the persecuted."

What are the reflections of an American on an occurrence like this? What must they be to one who has ever felt his pride of country stir within him, when in foreign lands he has beheld the degraded slaves of despotism bow in like manner before the altars and idols of heathenish superstition, awed into seeming reverence by the *military array* which always accompanies the imposing ceremonial of the Popish church?

But the military were only *a guard of honor!* Yes, this is the soft name given to this despotic chain, the musical sound to charm us away from scrutinizing it, and it will be sufficient, doubtless, to drown its harsher clanking in our torpid ears.

The *guard of honor*, that universal appendage of kings and sacred despots, is a serviceable band. It not only helps to swell a procession by its numbers, but with the glitter of its arms, and accoutrements, and gay banners, it adds splendor to the pageant of a heathen ritual.

But, reader, it has an essential duty to perform. *Its duty is to enforce the ceremonies of worship upon all present.* Do you doubt this duty of the guard of *honor?*

The writer will give his own experience of the duties of the guard of honor:

> I was a stranger in Rome, and recovering from the debility of a slight fever, I was walking for air and gentle exercise in the Corso, on the day of the celebration of the Corpus Domini. From the houses on each side of the street were hung rich tapestries and gold embroidered damasks, and

APPENDIX A

towards me slowly advanced a long procession, decked out with all the heathenish paraphernalia of this self-styled church. In a part of the procession a lofty baldechino, or canopy, borne by men, was held above the idol, the host, before which, as it passed, all heads were uncovered, and every knee bent but mine.

Ignorant of the customs of heathenism, I turned my back upon the procession, and close to the side of the houses in the crowd (as I supposed unobserved), I was noting in my tablets the order of the assemblage.

I was suddenly aroused from my occupation, and staggered by a blow upon the head from the gun and bayonet of a soldier, which struck off my hat far into the crowd.

Upon recovering from the shock, the soldier, with the expression of a demon, and his mouth pouring forth a torrent of Italian oaths, in which *il diavolo* had a prominent place, stood with his bayonet against my breast.

I could make no resistance, I could only ask him why he struck me, and receive in answer his fresh volley of unintelligible imprecations, which having delivered, he resumed his place in the *guard of honor*, by the side of the officiating cardinal.

Americans will not fail to observe in the precious extract of the discourse in which the priest gives vent to his feelings of exultation upon seeing our *national flag*, the star-spangled banner, humbled in the dust before the Pope, that with the cunning of his craft he flatters the soldiery, and in a sermon professedly to the God of Peace, and in dedicating a temple to his name, he is inspired with no loftier feelings of soul than this: "it would be *the pride of my soul*, to take the brave men by the hand, by whom these cannons were served."

Why? Is it such a brave act to touch off a cannon? Or was the imagination of the priest revelling in the dream of seeing the military power of the country, at a future day, at the beck and service of the Pope, and his Austrian master?

Appendix B

The Mask Thrown Aside

A charge of hostility to American institutions, against any sect or class in the community, is a very serious one, and only requires evidence to support it, to draw upon all its doings the watchful eye of American freemen. Is it asked, what evidence should you think sufficiently strong to substantiate the charge? I answer, the general principles of the sect would be sufficient, but its own declarations of hostility would certainly substantiate the charge.

If a Presbyterian journal, in commenting on the trial of the rioters at Charlestown, should make remarks like the following, the evidence would doubtless be considered complete:

> A *system of government* which admits a feeling of alarm in the execution of the laws from the vengeance of the mob, which Mr. Austin" (the prosecuting attorney) "distinctly allows to be the case—a vengeance exhibited by letters to the public officers and threats to the public authorities— *may be very fine in theory, very fit for imitation on the part of those who seek the power of the mob in contradistinction to justice and the public interest, but it is not of a nature to invite the reflecting part of the world, and shows at least that it has evils.* A public officer in England, who would publicly avow such a fear of executing his duty and carrying into effect the law of the realm, ought and would be thrust out of office by public opinion. *This one fact is condemnation* OF THE SYSTEM OF AMERICAN INSTITUTIONS, *confirmed lately by numerous other proofs.*

Appendix B

Now, could hostility to our institutions be more strongly expressed? And were Presbyterians or any other Protestant sect, thus boldly to avow its political antipathies, every political journal would seize upon this evidence of treason, and trumpet it through the whole country.

Why then are they now silent? This treason is actually uttered, nor is it less humiliating, or less dangerous that it is flung in our faces by a set of foreigners in the employment and pay of a foreign government, instead of native citizens.

The very words I have quoted are from the *Catholic Telegraph*, a Roman Catholic journal, edited and published at Cincinnati. Let it be borne in mind too, that a Catholic journal is under the supervision of the Bishops, who exercise a rigid censorship over it, that it speaks the authorized sentiments of the sect, and we shall then perceive something of the importance to be attached to these anti-republican declarations. They are indeed a precious, an invaluable testimonial to the *people*, of the duplicity of their professed friends. Everywhere in the land hitherto, Papists have been loudest in *professions* of attachment to American republican institutions.

They have now thrown off the mask. They unblushingly declare, that *"our system of government, though very fine in theory, is not of a nature to invite the reflecting part of the world,"* in short, that it is an experiment that has failed; that *"American institutions stand condemned by a single fact in the trial in Boston, and by numerous other proofs."*

And what has brought out this precious confession; what has occurred to make it a fit time to lay aside the disguise in which they have till now deceived the democracy of the country? What has produced this sudden revolution in their opinion of our form of government? Let us look into this matter.

A body of native citizens is excited to indignation by rumors (whether true or false alters not the case) that an act of foul play, such as the history of those nuisances (convents) in all countries have abundantly furnished, had occurred in the Charlestown nunnery.

This mob, instead of being met with efforts to appease it by immediate explanation, as would have been the case in any Protestant seminary in the land (for Protestants have no secret mysteries in their discipline), this mob, I say, is kept for days in an excited state by mysterious maneuvering, on the part of the Catholics, and by irritating threats from the Superior of the Convent, that, 20,000 foreigners under the orders of the Bishop would take vengeance upon the citizens, if they dared to commit any injury upon the Convent, and this threat was uttered *in sight of Bunker Hill*. Under this provocation the outrage was committed.

And is it a matter of surprise? I know of no one who justifies the illegal violence in burning the Convent, but I unhesitatingly say, that the feeling of indignation which animated the populace, was a just and proper feeling. It was roused by the belief that a young and helpless female had been illegally and cruelly abducted from her friends, and subjected to a secret tyrannical punishment.

The feeling, I say under this belief, was not only honorable to the Charlestownians, but, had they viewed such an outrage with indifference, they would have shown themselves unworthy of American citizens. Their error (and it cannot be defended, however it may be *palliated* by the gross insult which they received) consisted in suffering their just indignation to flow in an illegal channel, and instead of rallying round the laws, and strengthening them by a strong expression of public opinion at a special meeting of citizens, they leaped the bounds of law and committed a crime which the Papists are trying every possible means to cause to react in their favor.

But allowing that no palliating circumstances attended the act of the rioters, that no excuse could be pleaded for them as acting under the impulse of the most stinging insult that could be given to any people by a foreigner, what have these acts to do with our "system of government," or with "American institutions"?

In England, forsooth, they manage things better. There are never riots in England! London, Manchester, Bristol, I suppose were never agitated by riots! Paris, Lyons, Marseilles, Nismes, St. Petersburg, Brussels, Frankfort, Rome, Constantinople. None of these places under various systems of government, are ever witnesses to riots!

But this Popish enemy to our institutions may say, it is not the riot but the threatening letters sent to the prosecuting attorney to intimidate him in his duty, that tells against the government. Indeed, and who wrote the letters? Is it quite certain that they were not the production of some Jesuit to fan an excitement which was so likely to be turned to the advantage of his schemes?

Threatening letters are much in use in a certain Catholic country called Ireland, under a monarchical system of government. But suppose these letters were not written by Jesuits, but were the production of some wicked, or thoughtless person, what then? Is our form of government the cause of the writing of anonymous threatening letters? Would any other form of government prevent this evil of so alarming magnitude in the eyes of the *Catholic Telegraph*? Can it be prevented in England, or in any other form of government in the world?

Yes, there is one government which could probably prevent it. It is one in which the *Inquisition* is established, and by means of which, aided by the *confessional*, all that is considered necessary for the *good of the church*, could be brought to light, or rather to the ears of those most interested in knowing all secrets that bear upon their own power. How soon we shall be prepared for such a change of government to suit the designs of these busy, foreign emissaries, depends on the continuance of the character for sagacity, intelligence, and virtue of the American people.

Whatever doubts some may have hitherto had in regard to the existence of a foreign conspiracy in the country, I think the case is now become too plain to need further proof. Indeed, so bold are these foreign emissaries in the utterance of their anti-republican dogmas, so unblushing in their attacks upon our institutions, that we are often led to exclaim: What does this mean? Are these men fools, or madmen? Or are they so strong in their support from abroad, that they feel secure in bearding American freemen in their own homes?

The latter supposition alone satisfactorily explains their conduct. Austria is now playing a desperate game against liberty, for the safety of her own throne, and for that of her allies. It is the last hazard, and her object is gained if she can destroy the influence of our prosperity upon the people of Europe, a prosperity the natural result of our popular free institutions; and this latter object is effected, if, *by any means*, no matter how, riot and disorder can be produced in this country, to be pointed at as the effect of republican government.

Americans! Friends to liberty! Friends of order! Examine this subject, and decide with your usual sagacity and discretion. You have a busy, a crafty, a powerful, a dangerous set of foreign leaders, controlling and commanding a foreign population, ignorant and infatuated, intermixed with your own population, and who at a single signal from the Pope or from Metternich when the cause of despotism shall require the deed, can spread disorder and riot through all your borders.

Shrink not, Americans, from looking at the truth. You may boast of your peace and prosperity: *you hold them both, at this moment, at the mercy of Austria!* She has a disciplined band of foreigners in the midst of you, who in any season of excitement, she can make to fill your streets and dwellings with fear and confusion.

She may not think it prudent or expedient just now to exercise her power, but she has the power, through Popish priests, *who hold in check, at their pleasure, the elements of discord,* and whose favor you are compelled humbly to conciliate *as the price of your tranquility.* And this power is daily increasing, not merely by foreign immigration, and foreign money, but, with the deepest shame be it spoken, by the assistance, direct and indirect, of Protestant Republican Americans, who, with a facility most marvelous, fall into every snare and pleasant baited trap that Popery spreads for them.

☦

As the last sheet was printing, an article of intelligence was received, bearing importantly on the subject of this volume. Bishop England, the busy Jesuit whom I have had occasion before to notice, has just put forth an address to his Diocese at Charleston, on his return from Europe, from which we make the following extracts:

> During my absence I have not been negligent of the concerns of this Diocese. I have endeavored to interest in its behalf *several eminent and dignified personages whom I had the good fortune to meet; and have continued to impress with a conviction of the propriety of continuing their generous aid, the administration of those societies from which it has previously received valuable succor. In Paris and at Lyons I have conversed with those excellent men who manage the affairs of the Association for propagating the Faith. This year their grant to this Diocese has been larger than usual. I have also had opportunities of communication with some of the Council which administers the Austrian Association; they continue to feel an interest in our concerns.*
>
> The Propaganda in Rome, though greatly embarrassed, owing to the former plunder of its funds by rapacious infidels, has this year contributed to our extraordinary

expenditure; as has the holy father himself, in the kindest manner, from the scanty stock which constitutes his private allowance; but which he economizes to the utmost for the purpose of being able to devote the savings to works of piety, of charity, and of literature.

The prelates of the Church of Ireland, are ready, as far as our hierarchy shall require their cooperation, to give to them their best exertions in selecting and forwarding from amongst the numerous aspirants to the sacred ministry that are found in the *island of saints* (Ireland), a sufficient number of those properly qualified to supply our deficiencies. I have had very many applications, and accepted a few, who, I trust, *have been judiciously selected.*

We have here additional confirmation, if any were wanted, that in countries where Church and State are closely united, and where consequently *every religious association* (totally unlike our religious associations, which have no connection with the government) is directly connected with political objects, there is a great and special effort making to effect certain objects in the United States.

We have no less than *three* great societies, all formed to operate on this country. THEY say *religiously*, but let Americans, who know that Austria makes no movement which is not intended for political effect, judge whether religious benevolence towards this benighted land, or a deeper and more earthly feeling of political self-preservation prompts her *"continued feeling of interest in our concerns."*

Appendix C

The rules of the Leopold Foundation, the letter of Bishop Fenwick, of Ohio, to the Emperor of Austria, and Prince Metternich's answer are appended

Rules of the institution erected under the name of the Leopold Foundation, for aiding Catholic missions in America, by contributions in the Austrian empire

1. The *objects* of the institution, under the name of the *Leopold Foundation* are, (a) To promote the greater activity of Catholic missions in America; (b) To edify Christians by enlisting them in the work of propagating the Church of Jesus Christ in the remote parts of the earth; (c) To preserve in lasting remembrance her deceased Majesty, Leopoldina, Empress of Brazil, born Archduchess of Austria.
2. The *means* selected to attain these ends, are *Prayer* and *Alms*.
3. Every member of this religious institution engages daily to offer one Pater and Ave, with the addition: *"St. Leopold! Pray for us,"* and every week to contribute a crucifix; and thus by this small sacrifice of prayer and alms, to concur in the great work of promoting the true faith. As, however, everyone is free to enroll himself in this society, he may also leave it at pleasure.
4. Every ten members shall appoint one of their number a Collector, to receive the weekly alms. The collector shall see that the small number of his company, after the death or removal of any, is filled up. The alms collected shall be paid monthly, by the collector, to the parish minister of his district.

Appendix C

5. Every parish minister shall pay over, as opportunity offers, the alms collected in the manner prescribed, to the deacon (in Hungary the vice archdeacon), and he to his most reverend ordinariate.
6. If anyone intends a greater sum for this pious end, and that to be paid at once, his alms may be given either to the parish minister, with his own inscription inserted in the rubric designed, or to the deacon (or vice-deacon), or immediately to the most reverend ordinariate.
7. The most illustrious and reverend lord bishops of the whole empire are fully authorized to forward the alms thus obtained, from time to time, to the central direction of this religious institution, at Vienna.
8. The central direction at Vienna undertakes the grateful office of carrying into effect this pious work, under the protection of his most sacred majesty, and in connection with Frederick Rese, now Vicar-General of the Cincinnati bishopric in North America, and of employing the funds in the most efficacious manner to promote the glory of God and true faith in Jesus Christ; so that the alms collected by means of the most reverend ordinariates, or those sent immediately to them, shall be conscientiously applied, and in the most economical manner, to the urgent wants of American missions, as they are made known by authentic accounts and careful investigation.
9. The central direction will see that all the members of the society, for their spiritual consolation, and in reward for their pious zeal, shall be constantly informed of the progress and fruits of their munificence, as well as of the state of the Catholic Religion in America, according to the accounts received.
10. The Leopold Foundation, being a private religious institution, the central direction will solemnly celebrate the feast of the immaculate conception of the Blessed Virgin, the universal patroness of all religious assemblies, as the feast of the Foundation; but will also celebrate the feast of St. Leopold Marchion, the given name of the Empress Leopoldina and special patroness of this institution; and also every year on the 11th of December (the anniversary day of the death of Leopoldina, Empress of Brazil), it will see that the solemn mass for the dead be said for the repose of her soul, and all the souls of the deceased patrons and benefactors of the institution called by her name, all the members being invited to unite their pious prayers with the prayers of the Direction.

11. His Holiness, Pope Leo XII, eleven days before his most pious death, having declared his approbation of the institution (which must serve as a great incitement to all good Christians) did grant to its members large indulgences, in an express letter, the publication of which, being graciously permitted by his majesty on the 14th of April, was made by the most reverend ordinariates, to wit: "full indulgence to each member on the day he joins the society, also on the 8th December, also on the day of the feast of St. Leopoldina, and once a month if through the former month he shall have daily said a Pater and Ave, and the words: *Sancte Leopolde! Ora pro nobis* (St. Leopold, pray for us), and on condition that after sincere confession he partake of the sacrament of the Holy Eucharist, and pray to God in some public church for the unity of Christian princes, the extirpation of heresies, and the increase of Holy Mother church."
12. The most serene and eminent Arch Duke Cardinal Rudolphus, Archbishop of Olmutz, has kindly taken the supreme direction of the Leopold Foundation, and appointed the most high and reverend lord prince archbishop of Vienna his locum tenens. Vienna, 12 May, 1829.

The Pope's Letter of Approbation

The following is the letter of approbation of Pope Leo XII referred to above:

> *Be it remembered*, although there are many things which disturb and grieve our mind in the most weighty discharge of our apostleship, while we learn that some are not only opposed to the Catholic religion, but seek to draw others also into error; yet the God of all consolation does not suffer us to be without solace, but alleviates the labors, cares, and anxieties which we continually bear.
>
> This has recently happened, and we are filled with the highest joy, on hearing that in the kingdom of our well beloved son in Christ, Francis I., Emperor of Austria and King of Hungary, a society has been formed called the "Leopold Foundation," which is designed to aid the cause of missions.

For what is more useful to a Christian community, what is more excellent than by the preaching the word of God to confirm the just, and to lead the wandering from the paths of vice to those of salvation?

And indeed, as the Apostle says, "How shall they believe on him of whom they have not heard? And how shall they hear without a preacher, and how shall they preach except they be sent?"

We, therefore, desiring to favor, as far as God permits, such a society, do with a ready and willing mind grant the requests which have been made for the endowment of the same with some holy indulgences.

Therefore, trusting in the mercy of Almighty God, and the authority of Peter and Paul, his apostles, we grant to all the truly penitent cooperators in this society, who shall confess their sins, and partake of the feast of the Lord's body on the day on which they shall be received into the society, full indulgence and remission of all their sins.

Also, we grant full indulgence to them after they shall have been cleansed from the pollutions of life by holy confession, and received the Eucharist, on the 8th day of December, also on the day of the feast of St. Leopold, and once every month, provided that every day during the previous month they shall have said the Lord's prayer, the salutation of the angel, and the words, "St. Leopold, pray for us," and in some public church have said pious prayers to God for the harmony of Christian princes, the extirpation of heresies, and the glory of Holy Mother Church.

These letters we endow with perpetual efficacy; and we order that the same authority be given to the copies of them, signed by the public notary, and sealed with the seal of the person of proper ecclesiastical dignity, as is given to our permission in this very diploma.

Dated at Rome, at St. Peter's, under the ring of the fisherman, on the 30th day of January, 1829, in the sixth year of our Pontificate.

T. Card. Bernetti.

This apostolic letter is sanctioned by the royal leave.
By his Sacred Imperial Royal Majesty,
VICENTIUS SCHUBERT.
Vienna, 20th April, 1829.

First Report of the Leopold Foundation in the Austrian Empire, for the Support of Catholic Missions in America

The members of the Leopold Foundation are united to aid, by their prayers and their contributions, the messengers of God in America, in building churches, founding cloisters, establishing schools, and in providing all that is essential for the performance of divine worship.

We shall give a view of what the Leopold Foundation has done from its establishment to the end of October, 1830; then will follow accounts from the missions.

The institution went into operation on the 13th of May, 1829. The constitution, and the addresses delivered on the day of its establishment, were translated into the different languages of our monarchy, and sent in great numbers to the various dioceses, to give publicity to the undertaking.

In Vienna, an office was opened, which was given to the society free of rent by the Prior of the Dominicans. The result soon appeared in contributions from all quarters to the central treasury, exhibiting a lively proof of the zeal and efforts of priests and people to advance the kingdom God on earth.

Before giving a statement of the receipts and expenditures, we cannot withhold the letter which the pious bishop of Cincinnati, in North America, Mr. Edward Fenwick—whose Vicar-General, Frederick Rese, as is known to you all, by his visit to Vienna, gave occasion to the formation of our pious society—wrote to his majesty, our all-gracious Emperor, who had patronized the Society of the Leopold Foundation, together with the answer which in the name of his Majesty was given by his Serene Highness, the Chancellor of State, Prince Metternich.

Appendix C

Letter of the Bishop of Cincinnati to his Majesty, the Emperor of Austria:

CINCINNATI, 15th January, 1830.

SIRE,

May it please your Majesty to receive the most respectful homage of a man who is penetrated with feelings of gratitude for the good will and distinguished zeal of your Imperial Majesty, for the Catholic religion.

We feel ourselves irresistibly led to express to your Imperial Majesty, the consolation derived by the assembled bishops and directors of missions in America, at the recent news, that in the states of your Imperial Majesty, a society has been formed for the support of Catholic Missions in America.

We have the pleasure also to mention the safe return of our friend and Vicar-General, Mr. Frederick Rese, whose apostolical labors and unwearied zeal are above all praise. He brings me the most gratifying accounts of the kindness with which he was received and honored by pious and distinguished persons in your imperial city, especially of the flattering kindness with which he was received by your Imperial Majesty, who was pleased to lend your protection to the pious work of supplying the pressing wants of our poor missions, and our new diocese.

We venture here to flatter ourselves that the worthy inheritor of the virtues of St. Leopold and the great empress Maria Theresa, will continue to support us in our weak endeavors to extend the Catholic religion in this vast country, destitute of all spiritual and temporal resources, especially among the Indian tribes, who form an important part of our diocese.

We will not fail, daily to offer up our poor prayers to the Lord of Hosts, the king of heaven, that he may shed his richest blessings upon your Imperial Majesty, your illustrious family, and your whole kingdom.

Be pleased to accept graciously this expression of the sincere gratitude and reverence with which we subscribe ourselves your Imperial Majesty's most grateful, most humble, and most obedient servant.

EDWARD FENWICK,
Bishop of Cincinnati and Apostolical Administrator of Michigan, in the Northwest Territory.

Answer of his Serene Highness, Prince Metternich, Chancellor of State of his Imperial Majesty:

VIENNA, April 27, 1830.

Most worthy Bishop!

The Austrian consul-general at New York forwarded me the letter which your grace directed to the Emperor, my most illustrious master, on the 15th of January of this year. I did not delay to give it to his Majesty, who was highly gratified with the sentiments expressed in it, and commissioned me to answer your grace.

The Emperor, firmly devoted to our holy religion, feels a lively joy at the account that the truth makes rapid progress in the vast countries of North America. Convinced of the irresistible power which the Catholic doctrine must necessarily have on simple and uncorrupted hearts and minds, when its truths are proclaimed by truly Apostolical missionaries, his Imperial Majesty cherishes the most favorable hopes of the pious progress which our holy religion will make in the United States and among the Indian tribes.

The Emperor commissions me to say to your grace, that he cheerfully allows his people to contribute to the support of the Catholic churches in America, according to the plan laid down by your worthy vicar-general, Mr. Frederick Rese.

While I discharge myself of the commission of my illustrious master, to your grace, I feel happy in being his organ, and beg you to accept the assurance of the sentiments of respect and esteem, with which I remain, your grace's most humble and most obedient servant,

PRINCE VON METTERNICH.